# When a Sentence Ends in a Surprising Gazebo

# When a Sentence Ends in a Surprising Gazebo:

Stories and Poems from
826 Seattle Writing Workshops

Copyright © 2009 826 Seattle
When a Sentence Ends in a Surprising Gazebo: Stories and
Poems from 826 Seattle Writing Workshops
All rights reserved.

No part of this book may be reproduced in any form, or by any
electronic, mechanical or other means, without permission in
writing from the publisher.

Printed by United Reprographics

ISBN 0-9779832-6-9
Published by:

826 Seattle
8414 Greenwood Avenue North
P.O. Box 30764
Seattle, Washington 98113
(206) 725-2625
www.826seattle.org

Dedicated to helping young people improve their expository
and creative writing skills through free tutoring, mentoring,
workshops and other writing programs.

Special thanks to Amazon.com
for helping fund this project.

**amazon**.com

# Table of Contents

Foreword     xv
*Lemony Snicket*

## Earth of Beautiful Rejoicing

The Silver Bird     3
*Megan Jenkins*

The Fracas Fighters     7
*Alex Ronsse-Tucherov*

Me     13
*Cole Rowley*

Samuel el Civil     15
*Gabe Honeycutt*

The Moon     21
*Zoë Rogan*

## The Million Dollar Chandelier Shimmered

Frozen Dreams     25
*Salma Mahmoud*

Zombie Attack!     31
*Susana Kimble*

Animal Crossings     37
*Aislinn Leinster*

Double Doors: Three Sets     41
*Annie Bentley*

A Reflection of Myself     45
*Lucia Minahan*

## I Can Sleep Like a Feather in the Deep

### Poems — 49
*Jesa Chiro*

### I Am — 53
*Aliyah Rain Newman*

### The Music Does Not Have to Stop — 55
*Hailey Spencer*

### Deus ex Machina — 63
*Isabel Canning*

## What a Beautiful Language

### The Confidence Trials: A Modern Odyssey — 69
*Alice Mar-Abe*

### Sunnah's Time Capsule — 75
*Sunnah Rasheed*

### Bringing Stacey Home — 79
*Shamile Aldossary*

### Bubba — 91
*Rammah Elbasheer*

### Knowing — 95
*Kyrie Scarce*

## Salt Water was Mixing in with Brook Water

### The Boy at Bubble Brook — 99
*Zoë Rogan*

### So You Think You Can Tell Heaven From Hell — 103
*Fate Syewoangnuan*

| | |
|---|---|
| The Round House<br>*Oscar White* | 111 |
| Grandma's Special Soup<br>*Maggie Grasseschi* | 115 |
| Atlantis Reborn<br>*Josh Abrahamson* | 117 |

## A POTENT ENOUGH CURSE IN A LONG-FORGOTTEN FRENCH DIALECT

| | |
|---|---|
| This is Just to Say<br>*Lucia Minahan* | 129 |
| Who's the Outlaw?<br>*Yomna Anan* | 131 |
| Zucchini, The Dreaded Curse<br>*Kelson Ball* | 135 |
| Brains and Blood<br>*Declan Kimble* | 139 |
| Zombie Apocalypse in Port Salmon<br>*Ben Griggs* | 143 |

## BALLOONS WERE FALLING IN A CASCADE OF COLORS

| | |
|---|---|
| The Honeybee Tree<br>*Oscar White* | 149 |
| The Mombie<br>*Sean Huberth* | 151 |
| Water<br>*Chloe Noonan* | 155 |

| | |
|---|---|
| The S'more-tainous Monster<br>*Oliver Cauble* | 159 |
| Babette's Tale<br>*Jasmine Sun* | 163 |
| Fibonacci: Code of Life and Crime<br>*Sahl Ali* | 167 |
| Afterword<br>*Megan Burbank* | 183 |
| Acknowledgements | 187 |
| About 826 Seattle | 191 |

# Foreword

*Lemony Snicket*

*Is this a good book?*
Since the dawn of literature, readers have been asking themselves this question, and it is an important one. A book you haven't read might feel to you like a dog with which you are not acquainted. You might look into its eyes and see if it appears to be friendly. You might watch other people around the dog, to see if they are enjoying themselves. And you might take note of the dog's breeding and history, so that you might see if it has proven to be a good dog in the past. But eventually you will need to walk up to the dog and introduce yourself, and only then will you know whether the dog will become your faithful and true companion for the rest of your life, or whether it will chew off your arm, make a mess on your rug, and leave you terrified of dogs for the rest of your life. There are many people who are afraid to try new books, because so many of them have proven to be terrible house pets, and so just comfort themselves with things they have read before, like *Pat The Bunny* or a newspaper clipping about a rodeo murder that happened long ago.

As it happens, however, there is an elegant and foolproof system for determining whether or not a book is good, a system I developed myself after too many evenings in which I tucked myself into bed with a glass of water for refreshment, a pencil for taking notes, and a book I had never read, all set for a few hours of happiness, only to find myself rising from bed ten minutes later to throw the book out of the window because it was so irritating.

My system simply identifies thirteen surefire signs of an excellent book, so a book that has all thirteen signs is most certainly an excellent book, a book that has most of the thirteen signs is probably an excellent book, a book that has half the signs is iffy, and a book that contains few or none of the thirteen signs—such as any of the books I have written, by the way—is either a lousy book or not a book at all. I will share all thirteen signs with you, as you may be wondering this very moment whether or not the book you are reading now is any good, so that you may enjoy unalloyed textual bliss, a phrase which here means "a nice night reading, rather than needing to explain to your neighbors why there is a pile of discarded books outside your bedroom window."

**Sign #1: Nobility of intent.** "Nobility of intent" is a somewhat fanciful phrase which here means that the book has been written for a good purpose, unlike books that are written to insult individuals, or to stick under closet doors so that people cannot open them. This book benefits 826 Seattle, a noble institution indeed.

**Sign #2: Zombies.** A zombie is a dead person who, due to supernatural influence, is back amongst the living for the purposes of terrorization. Like many things in this world, a zombie is no fun in real life, but always improves a book. There are quite a few zombies in this book, the ones in the story "Zombie Apocalypse in Port Salmon" by Ben Griggs being the easiest to spot.

**Sign #3: A young author or authors.** There are, of course, plenty of very good books written by authors who are not young, but the advantage of a book with a young author or authors is that you can eagerly anticipate the long literary career they likely have ahead of them. The authors of this book are all tutoring students at 826 Seattle, which means they are all young, because older people are not offered tutoring, which is why I cannot speak German or play the zither.

**Sign #4: Maple syrup.** This particular sign is self-evident, a word which here means "easy to understand, because if a pancake is improved by maple syrup, then obviously a narrative would be." Gabe Honeycutt's story "Samuel el Civil" contains maple syrup in the world of espionage, a surprising and most welcome development.

**Sign #5: Breadth of imagination.** Dreadful books often display a woeful lack of imagination, dwelling on the same topics and themes over and over, such as "family joy" or "terrible things happening over and over to orphans." This particular book suffers from no such rut.

**Sign #6: Reference to the poetry of William Carlos Williams.** Everyone knows that books referencing this giant of American verse are better than books that do not. You probably will not have any trouble spotting this book's most obvious reference to Williams's poetry, but if you do, here is a hint: "Lucia Minahan."

**Sign #7: Suspense.** This book contains a great deal of suspense, a word which here means "narrative tension due to not knowing what will happen next." It is always interesting when a story ends in a surprising way, just as it is always interesting when a sentence ends in a surprising gazebo.

**Sign #8: A chicken as a hero.** Leo Tolstoy, one of the greatest writers in the world, missed a chance to make his classic novel Anna Karenina even better when he decided that the character of Count Alexei Kirillovich Vronsky should be an army officer, whose impetuous romanticism is Karenina's undoing even as it serves as a poignant reminder of the moral tempest of Russia in the late 19th century, rather than a chicken known for eating gravel. Jasmine Sun makes no such mistake.

**Sign #9: The name "Oscar White."** Although Oscar White is a young author (please see Sign #3), I am convinced that his name appearing in a book automatically guarantees its quality. If you do not believe me, check the table of contents of this book.

**Sign #10: Short chapters.** A book with long chapters can be very trying, because when you flip ahead to see how long the next chapter is, you are likely to decide to get a good night's sleep. This book has many short chapters, so I kept saying to myself, "I'll just read one more," and before I knew it I had stayed up all night finishing it and found myself in a state of delirium, a phrase which here means "so tired the next day that I decided to stay in bed eating cookies and reading it again."

**Sign #11: Goes well with cookies.** Please see Sign #10.

**Sign #12: The phrase "formerly blue dress."** All authors have authors they envy. F. Scott Fitzgerald supposedly envied Ernest Hemingway because Hemingway was prolific, a word which here means "very quick at writing." H.P. Lovecraft likely envied P.G. Wodehouse because Wodehouse was beatific, a word which here means "very, very happy." I certainly admire Zoë Rogan because Rogan is terrific, a word which here means "the inventor of the delightful literary phrase *'formerly blue dress.'* "

**Sign #13: A philosophically sound introduction by a writer of integrity and aplomb.** Modesty prevents me from writing anything further.

EARTH OF BEAUTIFUL REJOICING

# The Silver Bird

*Megan Jenkins*

Earth of departed sunset!
Earth of the shining full moon tinged with blue
Earth of shine and dark mottling the tide of the river
The Earth is rejoicing
Roses of pinks and yellows and whites and reds are
    celebrating spring
The blue sky has no gloomy gray
Then suddenly, as if in a dream
Everything disappears
And the world is sad and all the suffering you've never
    seen is there

Then I see a majestic silver bird swooping over the sad city
I follow
And find myself in a world of emerald leaves
Golden suns and blue magnificent waterfalls
I settle down in a rose garden
Full of yellows and pinks and reds
And I know the world is happy
All animals meet and are peaceful
From tigers and hens
To dogs, cats, and fish
All together where everyone is happy
Everything is always happy until you wake up

From a dream
But in your imagination dreams never end
You'll meet new friends and old friends and friends
    in between
And all this time you'll see beauty
Earth of friendship and joy
The Earth is still rejoicing
Crystal clear waters
Ruby-colored flowers and amethyst-colored flowers
And emerald leaves
Wonderful happiness and peace
And beauty all because of the silver bird who brought
    me here

Earth of beautiful rejoicing!
Earth of every tree
I start in New York and I fly to the Arctic and lovingly
    fold my laundry
I go and I swim to Hawaii
And playfully pet my cat
I remember the scary, scary moment when I saved
    my sister's life
But then I remember the fun, wonderful time at
    Emily's wedding reception
When I danced and danced all night
I remember the pain of the forty-four bobby pins
And the blood from my knee to my ankle

I remember good times and bad times
But the good times best of all
I remember love and hate
And pain and sadness

I am me and I love to be me
There are many different me's, all like snowflakes
Each and every one is different
I know who I am and where I belong
Because all of them are special
I miss Hannah and Ce-Ce and Lily
And Sydney, Maxence, Kendall, Eleanor
And all of my friends
The silver bird takes me to them
Everyone is happy.
And then he takes me home.

# The Fracas Fighters

*Alexander Ronsse-Tucherov*

## Chapter 1

On the north side of the tiny isle of Fracas, Namrak was picking apples for cider. Namrak's metallic blue eyes went wide with shock when a small, black spaceship suddenly appeared, crushing a nearby tree as it crashed, instead of landing smoothly. Namrak slowly stepped back as he watched the landing fins dig into the ground. The black hull of the ship was shaped like a dome. Strangely, it did not gleam in the bright daylight. A long staircase extended from the ship, and figures with smooth grey skin descended. The aliens looked around with menace in their catlike eyes. Namrak grabbed his ancient work jacket and ran as fast as he could to town.

Namrak quickly reached the armory on the edge of Town Square. He burst through the door shouting, "There is an alien invasion going on! What do you have to stop it?"

The armory shopkeeper started, and said to Namrak, "I always wondered when this day would come—when our universes would cross," he shuddered. "How about a Portable Electric Immobilizing Pulser, only $19.95."

"I'll take it!" Namrak said, grabbing the PEIP and heading out the door.

Outside, he saw the aliens enter the Buy-Stuf-Now on the other side of Town Square. He raced into the supermarket, where he saw several aliens roaming the aisles along with crowds of cowering people. The aliens were wielding strange blue guns. He spotted an alien about to shoot a clerk who had slick, black hair. Namrak quickly zapped the alien, who froze in place, then proceeded to zap the rest of the aliens in the store before they could harm anyone. Then, Namrak jumped onto the slick-black-haired clerk's checkout stand and cried out, "We need to fight the rest of these aliens! Who is with me?"

"I'm in!" said the clerk. "Name's Cronor. And thanks for saving me."

A young woman with straw-yellow hair stepped forward. "I'm Samantha, and I'll help too!"

Lastly, a gentleman in an expensive-looking dark brown suit joined the group. "You may call me Max, and I will also join your team."

Namrak jumped off of the checkout stand and smiled at Max, Samantha, and Cronor. "Let's get started on a plan."

## Chapter 2

The newly formed Fracas Fighters, armed only with Namrak's PEIP and four large security mirrors they had torn from the ceilings, prepared to leave the market. They needed to return to the armory, but thirty aliens in Town Square blocked their way.

The aliens shot liquid metallic blue laser beams at the team as they dodged across Town Square. A flurry of beams rushed toward the Fighters, only to be reflected back by the mirrors. The reflected beams disintegrated the aliens who had shot them, leaving piles of ash on the ground. Namrak shot back bravely, as he fearlessly led his team through the blazing laser blasts and into the Armory.

"We need bomb supplies NOW!" Namrak shouted as they burst through the door. Samantha and Max barricaded the door as Cronor and Namrak went up to the counter.

"I've got a 200-piece snap-together bomb kit," said the shopkeeper. "Today only, on sale for $10.99."

Namrak pulled a one-dollar bill from his pocket. "Darn, I spent almost all my money on the PEIP."

They all turned to look at Max. "Why are you looking at ME?"

Samantha snickered, "Well, look at your clothes, you dandy."

"I'm not THAT rich—this outfit is a rental," Max said sheepishly. But he did pull out a five-dollar bill and six ones from his silk-lined pockets. "Keep the change."

Everyone laughed as Max handed Namrak the money. "Great, we'd better get out of here and put this baby together. Or should I say Big Boy—I sure hope it lives up to its name and the hype on the box." The team grinned at each other with excitement. Just then the grey aliens burst through the barricade and the Fracas Fighters snuck out the back.

The foursome ran into the apple orchards, avoiding or PEIPing the aliens they saw along the way. In a small clearing they sat down and began to assemble the Big Boy bomb. "Hey, what goes between B12 and C9?"

"A7."

"Wow, wouldn't it be cool if it made sense how these should be put together?"

"Yeah, seriously!"

Suddenly, another spaceship landed in the clearing nearby. It looked almost exactly like the black spaceship that had crushed the apple tree, but it was silvery and gleaming. The team prepared to run, but there was no time. From THIS spaceship came normal-looking people, although they had the catlike eyes of the aliens. One of them stepped forward. He was wearing a beautiful white satin suit with a silken black tie. Namrak thought, Max would have lunged at this person if it weren't for that suit. I wonder if it's a rental, too.

The person in the suit said, "No, it isn't a rental, Namrak." Everyone jumped in surprise.

"I am Prince Aron III, and I hail from the planet of Manos. Please, let me explain what is happening.

"Our planet was in civil war, Manoses against the creatures known as Krothigers. The Krothigers made excess amounts of Adamanite, a crystallized mix of Adamantine and diamond. Adamanite has a unique metallic blue appearance. Adamanite has thousands of uses, including mind reading and explosion amplification. In fact, we got our special powers from Adamanite. The Krothigers used a seed of this crystal to help rip our planet in two, with us on one side, and the Krothigers on the other. Because Adamanite turns ash into more Adamanite, they started destroying planets in order to get huge amounts of Adamanite. We plan to stop the destruction here."

As he spoke, Prince Aron deftly assembled the problematic bomb. Then Aron handed Namrak a small device. "This will let you send messages to me using your mind, which I will respond to. I have inserted an Adamanite seed into your bomb. Also, replace those mirrors with these Adamanite shields." Aron pulled four large blue shields, seemingly out of thin air, and handed them to the party.

"Okay team, let's go!" Namrak called, and the Fracas Fighters took off.

## Chapter 3

The Fracas Fighters rammed into the Krothiger ship's door with their new Adamanite shields and, with much effort, broke it down. Once inside, Namrak thought, Where to?, and heard in his mind, The control room should be at the first right. Use your shield and you should walk out fine. Plant the bomb, then press the large red button right next to the steering wheel in the front of the room. This will set a delayed course to the Krothigers' home planet. Make sure to get all of the Krothigers with your PEIP, but don't hit the ship or it won't take off!

"This is it!" Namrak quickly turned the corner and began immobilizing the Krothigers ahead. Samantha set the bomb while Cronor pressed the autopilot button, and Max helped Namrak with the alien crew members. When the last alien was frozen, Namrak shouted, "Let's get out of here!"

The team jumped out of the ship. The vessel began to shake, slowly leaving the ground, until it zoomed quickly out of sight. Back at the Manoses' ship, the team saw Prince Aron waiting for them.

Prince Aron said, "Excellent work. Just…great job. I'll handle the Krothigers left behind. My team is already loading them into our ship. We are indebted to you, Fracas Fighters. We can stay in contact with you with that device in Namrak's pocket. I need to return home to report our success. My father will be so happy that the Krothigers' planet will be space pebbles."

The Fracas Fighters waved at the ship as it ascended to the skies. Namrak said to his buddies, "We really should stick together. We should be a permanent force." The team replied with a very solid YES.

The End…or is it?

# Me

*Cole Rowley*

I am a box of Legos, and I have been passed down from generation to generation. I am in Seattle, Washington. A boy named Phill used to own me. Once, he built a castle with a jail inside it. He looked like he was having fun with all of the Lego people inside of the castle. Phill grew up and passed on the Legos to Value Village. I was put on a shelf in the toy section where I was instantly bought.

# Samuel el Civil

*Gabe Honeycutt*

My name is Samuel el Civil . . . well, in reality, that is not my name, but it is all I can tell you because my real name is top secret. I am going to tell you a story about one of my missions called "Canadian Syrup."

One day I was called down to my agency, HQ 26, by my boss. I cannot tell you his name either, but he is a tall, plump man—and his cheeks swell up like apples all the time. That day he looked worried.

"Ah, Samuel," said my boss, "I need you to go on a mission."

"Well, sir, that's what we do here," I said.

"No time to be smart! The Canadians are planning to take over Greenwood, Washington D.C., and all of our syrup factories," said the boss.

I replied, "Sir, that's horrible news about Washington D.C. and Greenwood . . . but the syrup factories, that wouldn't be so bad."

"Samuel, you will go with Will. I'll need you to find their listening post and destroy it, then find their new weapon."

The next day I left the agency and got into the car; a new model called the Mega Car. It had SS thrusters, a red metal paint job, and a soda cooler. The soda cooler is great, even if it is not a missile launcher.

I met up with Will in Greenwood, at my favorite gelato

cafe. Will is in his twenties, and his hair has the color of strawberries—so he sticks out in a crowd. He has a muscular build, and stands at about six feet seven inches. Will's personality is that of a nice man—but if you mess with him, you'll get King Kong.

I first met Will when I was doing a mission in Finland. I was looking for some top secret plans in the U.S. ambassador's apartment when Will jumped out at me. He was planning to kill me, but then a man with a tazer jumped out from the door and shot at Will. I jumped in front of him, then when I woke up I was in a hospital. Since I basically saved his life, he and I are now friends.

"Hey, Sam, how's it doing?" said Will.

"I have a new mission. Come with me to get a new gadget," I said.

It had been shipped with a few other things. I started out the door when I heard gunfire! Two police officers fell dead in front of my feet, then two men came out of a door in the front of the store. I hid for cover.

"Eh, John where did he go?" said one of the men, who had an accent that sounded like he had butter in his mouth.

"Over there," said the tall man, who sounded like he had marbles in his mouth.

I ran behind one of the walls.

"THERE HE IS! SHOOT HIM NOW!" said the tall one.

The bullet grazed my arm. The door opened, and out came Will. BLAM! BLAM! He shot his pistol at the men, and one was killed; the other dodged the bullet.

"Well, Tom, you did always talk too much," the man said.

I grabbed him from behind. "Hey, you're not Canadian, you're English!" He hit me and ran.

"Forget about the gadget," said Will. "We need to go to the closed McDonalds before they come back with an armored car."

I went there and snuck in. I turned on my stealth helmet and I was able to see a radio and a laptop.

"Well, nobody's here," I said. Then I heard footsteps and hid. I pulled out my tazer and fired. Two men fell down. I snuck over to the radio and laptop—and as soon as I did—I felt a sharp needle hit my neck, and I fell unconscious.

When I awoke, I could see a huge ray gun in front of me. I was sitting in a long chair with claws at the top of it.

"Hello, Mr. Civil," said a man in a black tuxedo with blond hair and a twisted smile. He had a patch on his arm that said "England" on it, as did everybody else.

"Do you know that the Canadians have nothing to do with this?" he said. "Yes, in fact, they love your nation. It is the English that don't."

He told me his name was Burt. "Burt is a really cool name," I said.

"Wow, you think so?" said Burt.

"No, it stinks!" I responded.

"ANY LAST WORDS, MR. CIVIL?" yelled Burt.

"YEAH, eat pineapple!"

I tossed a small pineapple, which exploded in Burt's face.

"Mommy!" said Burt in pain. "SAY GOODBYE TO WASHINGTON, D.C.!"

I threw my pen at him, and smoke shot out of it! The ray gun exploded and maple syrup went everywhere.

"This is your weapon of mass destruction? A maple syrup gun?"

"Yes." said Burt, blushing.

After a day, all the maple syrup was cleaned up and

Burt and his men were arrested… so Washington D.C. and Greenwood were saved by a pen.

# The Moon

*Zoë Rogan*

A girl studied the dim stars and bright, pale moon. The scenery made her feel good. She stared up at the moon, and she heard the chirp of a cricket. She smelled the sweet scent of a flower. Her clothing was crisp, and smelled of peaches. She stood up, and skipped over to an apple tree and picked up the juiciest, crunchiest apple and took a bite. She retired back to her old position. She felt the grass tickle her arms. Then, after stargazing a bit more, she went inside.

# The Million Dollar
Chandelier Shimmered

# Frozen Dreams

*Salma Mahmoud*

The million-dollar chandelier shimmered as my stepsister, Erica, my older brother, Sebastian, and I entered my father's new hotel. My father married Catherine last year, just after my mother died of pneumonia. Catherine often followed my dad on business trips, which left Erica and me under Sebastian's supervision.

I had never really liked Erica. We had been in school together since second grade, but our parents met last fall at ninth grade curriculum night. Within a few months, they decided to get married. Erica was always popular. I was always shy. There was no way that we could be friends. Erica's smile could light up a whole town. Nobody could compare to her exquisite green eyes and silky blonde hair. Especially me.

When we walked up to the reception desk, Sebastian asked where my dad was. The receptionist told us that he had gone on a business trip and would be back by that night. Just then, the elevator opened and out walked my stepmother, Catherine.

Catherine quickly grabbed Erica and gave her a long hug accompanied by a compassionate speech explaining how much she missed her. Times like these really made me miss my mom. The two of them headed up to Erica's room to unpack. On the elevator up to our rooms, Sebastian cornered me.

"Ellie, something's bugging you. Tell me what's wrong," he said.

"Nothing's wrong. Everything's just fine."

"Trust me, I know when someone's feeling down. Tell me what happened."

I didn't know if I should tell him. I didn't want to complain about my problems to him, but I knew he'd keep asking until I told him.

"Okay, I'll tell you. Just don't tell anyone else," I said.

"Don't worry, I won't."

"I can't stand Erica. She's perfect."

"Ellie, she isn't better than you. Just choose something she doesn't like and stick to it. Try your best, and she won't be able to beat you at it."

"You know, Sebastian, I guess you're right." The problem was, I couldn't think of anything that I could do that Erica couldn't do better.

"I remember Mom was really good at ice-skating. Maybe I could try doing that," I said.

"Sure. I can take you to the skating rink today."

"Really? Thanks."

Within an hour, Sebastian managed to get a taxicab to drive us down to a newly opened ice-skating rink. He gave me fifty dollars to buy a new figure-skating dress and sat there for an hour as I skated. I remembered how I had always attended my mom's skating competitions. As soon as I stepped on the ice, I felt free. As the ice glimmered beneath my skates, I thought, maybe I'm better than I expected. I guess it just came naturally.

"Eleanor, all I can say is, you've got skill," said my brother as we rode back to the hotel.

When we arrived, I noticed Erica sitting down in the lobby. Her light-up-the-town smile wasn't shining as usual. When she saw me in my figure-skating dress, she asked where I had been.

"Erica, relax. Sebastian just took me to the ice-skating rink. Turns out, I'm actually pretty good," I said.

"Since when do you ice-skate?"

"I just decided to try today."

"Eleanor, you will never be a good ice skater no matter how hard you try. You'll just fail, the same way you do at everything else."

As my eyes began to water, I wondered why someone so perfect would get mad at me for trying something new.

Later that night while having dinner, Sebastian announced that he had signed me up for a skating competition the next day. I was completely speechless.

"What? That's not fair. I want to enter! Sign me up now!" said Erica.

I expected Sebastian to ignore her, but he didn't. He called the ice-skating place and told them to add another contestant to the list. I protested weakly, saying she didn't have a dress, but Sebastian ignored me.

The next morning, we all woke up and headed down to the skating rink. Once Erica decided to enter the competition, I was pretty sure that I was going to lose. After watching thirteen other girls perform, she was up. This was the first time I had ever seen her look so insecure. Right as she stepped on the rink, she slipped. As much as I hate to admit it, this actually made me more confident. When my skates finally touched the ice, I felt even more secure. I successfully landed a 180-degree turn. The judges looked amazed.

When I finished, the announcers came on. I hurried back

to my seat.

"It looks like our judges have decided on a winner," an announcer said.

"We are proud to present this gold trophy to Eleanor Coffrey!"

Everyone clapped. As I walked up to claim my trophy, I realized that I'd never been prouder of myself. I gave a short speech thanking everyone for being supportive, especially Sebastian. I even thanked Erica for motivating me. After all, I wouldn't have tried ice-skating in the first place if she weren't so perfect.

When I got offstage, Erica came to talk to me.

"Good job out there, Ellie. I'm sorry for trying to ruin it for you," she said.

"It's okay. I'm sorry we haven't been very great stepsisters."

"Maybe we should just end this feuding. Let's just be friends. Deal?"

"Deal. Thanks, Erica."

# Zombie Attack!

*Susana Kimble*

Things couldn't get any worse for Sally. Her cookie cart had only sold two cookies, her pet bunny had run away, Lilly had ditched her to go to the bowling alley, the ice cream truck didn't even come—and to make things worse—she had to miss the last screening of Harry Potter 5 . . . and they didn't even own a TV!

So there she was; sitting on her bed, staring at the wall where her best painting once hung. It was the one that had been ripped to shreds by her brother to make bedding for the bunny, and she had salvaged what remained of it anyway.

Her phone rang, and she picked it up.

"Hello," she said.

"Hi. It's Lilly. Sorry I bailed on you."

"Oh, you know, it's fine. You know, I only sold two cookies today. Wanna help?"

"Sure. Let's sell them by Camp Happiness. They just got out."

"But," said Sally, "that's by the graveyard."

"Oh, don't be such a scaredy-egg." Lilly said her words mockingly. "I'll be right over."

But when Sally hung up, she knew that something would go wrong.

\* \* \*

Creaaak... A noise came from the attic. Sally rolled over on her side and threw a glance at her clock: 12:01. The clock's angry red glare stared back at her. Sally groaned and shoved her face into her pillow. The attic creaked louder, and Sally heard a thump! She stepped out of bed, put her slippers on, and slipped out silently to see what was going on. Sally had memorized all the creaky spots in the floor, and walked silently up to the attic. An icy shiver ran down her spine. She was almost there... one more step!

A furry, dirty foot poked out of the dusty attic door. It was green, had split toenails, and some of them were even ripped off! Little clots of dirt were under its skin. Sally thought she could see maggots writhing inside. Pus-filled pockets bulged and burst on it.

Sally screamed! The foot disappeared, and Sally ran down the stairs. She came back up a minute later, a noodle strainer on her head, a cookie pan taped to her chest, a frying pan in one hand, and a potato peeler in the other. She slowly opened the door and peered inside... but there was nothing there, and no evidence that someone had been there, except a smashed window, the curtain blowing in the cool wind. Sally shivered again and went downstairs.

"That was creepy," she said to herself.

Suddenly she remembered: Mom and Dad! They would have gotten up if they had heard me scream!

She ran to their bedroom. The window was broken, and there was a familiar smell of rotting soil coming from the bed sheets. They were gone.

\*\*\*

Sally looked up and found it staring at her... but she couldn't actually tell if it was staring at her. Its glazed-over eyes didn't have pupils. She studied it and kept silent, hoping it wouldn't notice her. Its peeling, pusy, yellow-green skin looked to have maggots squirming under its decaying complexion. The same foot from the attic was now stepping on her toe. She winced with pain. She was still looking at its pupil-less eyes and wondered: Is it staring at me?

"Brains..." it said.

"Definitely!" Sally said, and dashed for the door.

As she went out, she thought: Did it follow me home from the graveyard after we sold the cookies?

She dashed outside with a fuse. Now she had a plan; one that she had figured out herself. She grabbed her oil and matches. The oil "glugged" out of the can as the zombie (or at least that's what she thought it was) followed. She set up the fuse . . . She lit it. The bubbling oil burned up the zombie! She breathed a sigh of relief.

Then she heard, "Brains..."

Then she heard it again . . . and again.

Thousands of zombies were pouring out of the graveyard, all walking directly to her! She pulled her backpack off her shoulders and unzipped it. She had a few foldable tubs and lots of salt. She quickly poured salt into the tubs (she had read in a book that salt can kill zombies). The zombies fell into the tubs. Suddenly, Lilly came up behind Sally riding a fifty-foot inchworm!

"Come on," she said. "Hop on."

After Sally hopped on, she yelled over the roar of the inchworm, "Where did you get this thing!?"

"Remember when we buried Inchie?!"

"Yeah!"

"Remember how we buried him by the nuclear power plant?!"

"Yeah!"

"It's been leaking! Go, Inchie go!"

Inchie bounded over houses and roared a triumphant roar. He squished hordes of zombies as the people of the town had all gathered to watch. Everyone was chanting as loud as they could: "GO, INCHIE GO! GO, INCHIE GO!"

Then Sally told Inchie quietly, "To the graveyard, Inchie."

Inchie roared, up on his hind legs, beating his feelers on his chest. Sally noticed a small boy clinging to one of Inchie's feelers for dear life!

"TOMMY!" she screamed.

Tommy crawled up the feeler and plopped himself down behind Sally.

"You aren't going to fight zombies without me!" He pulled out his clubs for the Wii game "Whack a Mole" and handed one to each of them.

"Inchie," he said calmly, "bring us down."

Inchie roared and sent out some five-foot inchworms. They hopped on and said "Thanks" to Inchie. Inchie clapped his feelers and waited at a nearby tree. They whacked and whacked at the zombies, until Tommy suddenly said, "That's fifty points for me!"

"Yeah, well, I got seventy-two!" Lilly yelled. She always enjoyed Sally's seven-year-old brother.

"Oh, yeah!?" Sally yelled, deciding to play along. "I got 124!"

"We have a winner!" Lilly yelled like a game show host. "Next round!"

They whacked until there were no more zombies. Tommy spread salt around the graveyard.

"156!" Tommy yelled.

"155!" Sally yelled.

"We have a winner!" Lilly yelled again, pointing towards Tommy.

Now, everything was back to normal.

(Except they kept Inchie.)

### Epilogue

Sally and Tommy found their parents back at home—they didn't remember a thing. In all the commotion, Lilly forgot all about her parents, and when she returned home they were dead... So Sally's family adopted her. They made a pen for Inchie in Sally and Lilly's room (they expanded it first). Every day Lilly and Sally ride Inchie to school, and he waits outside. Inchie has some friends, as they set up an inchworm riding school. He is pretty popular. Sally and Lilly have decided not to sell cookies by the graveyard EVER again!

# Animal Crossings

*Aislinn Leinster*

### Raccoon

People streamed through the double doors. A lady in a red dress yelled, "Ghost!" Ana, Holly, and Ava all turned in shock. Lightning struck. It was a dark and stormy night. The next day the girls went to the movie theater (that was where they had been last night) to see if there was a ghost. They looked everywhere; they were about to quit when Ava screamed, "Ghost!" Ana and Holly ran over to where Ava was, and there at the back of the movie theater, with his head stuck in a bag of popcorn, was a raccoon!

### Crocodile

People streamed through the double doors. Jack (a boy who sells newspapers) was used to this, but today was a lot different. Everyone was screaming! All the people rushed onto the train and yelled at the driver to go. The train rushed off. Jack looked through the double doors, and there he saw a huge crocodile! At first he was sure he was dreaming, because, one, there is no zoo close by, and, two, crocodiles don't live anywhere near here! But there it was, a huge crocodile! He was so scared, he ran off screaming!

### Tiger

As the tiger sneaks up on its prey, its tail flicks at lightning speed, its stripes move with its body like waves, its claws are out ready to strike, its eyes are glaring. He's down low, camouflaged in the grass; he's quite close now and he strikes; he fights for his meal. He is successful and satisfied.

### Cat

The cat purrs very, very loudly, gets started, and jumps out the door. It is a dark, dark night. The cat feels her way around the garden. She stops dead, feeling a raccoon is close. Her heart jumps, and she runs as fast as her legs can carry her. She is inside, safe and sound.

## Double Doors: Three Sets

*Annie Bentley*

People streamed through the double doors. All the little kids came in first, then the big kids. The food that Mrs. Pit made was the best food ever, and it was for school lunch! They never wanted food from home because Mrs. Pit made the best food ever. All kids, teachers, and staff loved her food. Mrs. Pit couldn't say a thing she was so excited. But one day a new cook came, so they all said they felt sick, but they weren't. After a whole month Mrs. Pit came back, and all the kids came back.

\*\*\*

People streamed through the double doors. They all began to race to the second double doors to catch the train to Iceland! All of a sudden the first person went all the way to the back, and the last person went to the front of the glob—then stopped! The next day they got on the twelve o'clock train. It was the weirdest thing ever.

\*\*\*

People streamed through the double doors. They were all trying to buy a new movie called The Grand Gem. The makers of The Grand Gem were trying to make money to make a big movie theater, and they needed wallpaper, paint, seats, floors, and things like that. But they didn't have enough money, so they put the movie in every store on Earth. They finally made enough money to get wallpaper, paint, seats, floors, and things like that. The new movie theater was called Dixe Movies.

# A Reflection of Myself

*Lucia Minahan*

I see a reflection of myself in a mirror on the wall. I stop and look to see my beautiful face looking right back at me. I know that even though I might feel bad or sad or mad I will always be loved. I know that God above me and Earth below me will always love me. And so will my mother and father, my aunt and uncle. I, Lucia, love animals from iguanas to zebras. I know my love for these animals will never retire, for love can never die, because even if your heart is broken the love will never pour out.

# I Can Sleep Like a Feather in the Deep

# Poems

## *Jesa Chiro*

1.
I see trees blowing in the breeze
I see mountains on hills
I hear waves crash and roar
I am here to see Earth doing its job
I am lying in the grass
I think I will do nothing for a long time
But listen to the breeze

2.
Writing and art are in your writing hand
Earth and magic are in your heart and brain
Power is in your feet

3.
I can be anything
I can fly like a magical pie
I can float like a boat
I can eat like a chimpanzee
I can sleep like a feather in the deep
I can say bye like a little fly

4.
The spring looks up at the moon
I look back
The stars twinkle at me
I twinkle back
The moon waves at me
I wave back
I close my eyes and dream about them

# I Am

*Aliyah Rain Newman*

I am a daughter
  Baking cookies with my mom
I am a sister
  Hiding and seeking with my brother
I am a cousin
  Playing dress-up in the afternoon
I am a niece
  Of a mother with a new son
I am a student
  Eating chocolate from my teacher
I am a granddaughter
  Tubing at my grandparent's lake house
I am a girl
  Cantering on ponies
I am me
  Sometimes, I just like to be alone.

# The Music Does Not Have To Stop

*Hailey Spencer*

Selena was in a dark room. A man was playing piano and the music was getting eerier and the man disappeared but the music was still playing and where was Charlene? Selena needed her help and it was getting darker and nobody would rescue her and what was going on and the music was getting louder what would happen when the music stopped and she didn't have a chair and—

"Selena?" Charlene's calm, soft voice broke through her dream state.

"What?" asked Selena, in a sharper tone then she had intended. She was confused to be awoken so suddenly, but incredibly relieved that the dream was over. Why wouldn't the dream stop coming?

"There's land up ahead. Should we stop there?"

Selena nodded.

\*\*\*

They docked their boat and walked on shore, into the mansion that dominated the island, right into Selena's nightmare. Only she could see the man at the piano more clearly, and this man had only one eye.

The Cyclops turned suddenly, clapped once, and said, "Guests!" The piano continued to play, although his hands were not on the keys.

\*\*\*

"You want us to help you destroy the Isle of Fijora?" Charlene cried, in incredulous outrage. How could this creature think that she and Selena would destroy their beautiful island?

"It is the only way," he replied, remorsefully. "They would have the music stop."

"What happens when the music stops?" Charlene asked, wondering what it could be that had given Selena that terrified look.

"I will show you," the Cyclops replied, about to take his hands off the piano once again, and this time, Charlene was sure that the music would not continue to play.

"No!" Selena shrieked. "Don't do it! Please don't!"

"Will you help our noble cause?"

"Never!" Charlene spat. "I don't trust you."

"Then I have no choice."

\*\*\*

Selena shivered in the cold darkness of the piano where the Cyclops had left them, willing herself not to cry. Tears are for the weak, she reminded herself.

"Charlene?" Selena's voice cracked slightly, but she ignored it. "What do you think will happen to us?"

Before Charlene had time to answer, a voice began to sing, and Selena and Charlene fell asleep.

Selena dreamed of two girls who were the same, but different, and were sometimes one. When she woke, she was swinging on a cloth hammock under a sea of fruit, swinging gently on tropical trees, and Charlene was nowhere to be seen.

\*\*\*

Charlene began to eat the sweet fruit hanging off the branches, and by the time her chin had become covered in juice, she had forgotten all about Selena. She had forgotten that she didn't know where she was or how she had gotten there. All she could remember was the fruit.

"Hello," said a small, sturdy girl, springing lightly out of a nearby tree. "What's your name?"

"I'm Charlene."

"Hello, Charlene."

\*\*\*

"You were in my dream," Selena accused the strange girl.

"My name is Aertra," she replied, piercing Selena with sharp, brown eyes.

"How did I get here?"

"You dreamed it, so it was so."

Selena stared at her with dread. "So I'll always have to live my dreams?"

"That's an interesting question," Aertra replied.

"Were you the one singing?"

"Yes and no." Aertra did not explain further. Selena continued asking questions, for she longed for answers.

"Are you a goddess?"

Aertra paused for a moment, and then said, "I am more—and less—than any goddess."

\*\*\*

"We don't have much time."

"Why?" Charlene asked the girl.

"You need to find your friend."

"You mean Selena?" Charlene asked, remembering.

"Yes."

"Why?"

The girl looked at her. "You love her. But it might be too late for her. She may have gone the wrong way. Find her. But be cautious. You have not reached your crossroads yet."

Charlene asked, without even thinking, "Are you a goddess?"

"I am more—and less—than any goddess. Find your friend."

Charlene blinked, and the girl was gone.

\*\*\*

"I don't understand," Selena said.

"Someone is coming. I must go."

Selena blinked, and Aertra was gone. A moment later, she heard the light sound of feet hitting the sand. Turning, she saw Charlene, and ran towards her.

"Where *were* you?" she demanded, trying not to show how worried she'd been.

"I don't know," said Charlene.

\*\*\*

Selena was walking, walking through the tall fruit trees, moving faster, faster, until she got to the shore and found their little rowboat waiting, She was walking towards it and—

Selena woke up.

"You can't stay forever," said a girl, walking out from the trees.

"Aertra?"

"You and I have not yet met."

"But you look just like her."

"I am Artrea. Aertra is my sister. Now, heed my words. You cannot stay forever. To do so would be perilous." She disappeared, leaving Selena wondering if she had dreamed the whole thing.

\*\*\*

"She's keeping secrets," whispered a voice in Charlene's ear. She sat up.

"You never told me your name," Charlene said.

"My name is Aertra," she replied.

"What secrets is Selena keeping?"

"That's an interesting question."

"Can she hear us?"

"She is not in our reality."

"What do you mean?" Charlene demanded.

"Too many questions. I have come to deliver a warning, so heed my words. You cannot leave here. To do so would be perilous." She disappeared, leaving Charlene wondering if she had dreamed the whole thing.

\*\*\*

When they awoke, neither Charlene nor Selena mentioned her mysterious visitor from the previous night. Selena, remembering the girl's warning, did tell Charlene of her dream, and her theory that they were on the same island they'd landed on. Charlene did not share her enthusiasm.

"I think we should stay here a little longer. We know it's safe here."

"No, we don't, and if you don't come with me, I'll leave alone." Selena would not waste time arguing.

"No, you can't!"

"I have to," said Selena, quite calmly. She knew that Charlene would not stay here and watch her row away.

\*\*\*

"The music does not have to stop," whispered Aertra. "You must follow our friend, the one who plays the music."

"The music must be stopped," whispered the other girl. "You must abandon the Cyclops, the one who is played by the music."

"Pick a card, Little One," and a deck appeared and Selena drew the Ace of Diamonds and Aertra—or the other one—said "You've chosen wrong," and the music stopped and Charlene got off her chair and gave it to Selena and Selena was selfish and sat and Charlene was dying but Selena was scared to leave her chair so she turned away and would not watch her friend die.

"Pick a card, Little One," and a deck appeared and Selena drew the Jack of Spades who has one eye—the one-eyed monster—and Aertra—or the other one—said "You've chosen right," and because she had drawn the right card Charlene would not die and the music would not stop.

Selena woke up.

\*\*\*

"So you don't work with the Cyclops?"

Lena shuddered. "Of course not! He's vile. I prefer to stay out of this sort of thing, so I may stay unnoticed."

"He noticed me and Selena."

"They desire the power that Selena has."

"You mean her dreams?"

Lena nodded. "I believe they have found a way to manipulate her dreams."

Charlene fell back against the soft couch pillows, exhausted. "You said that Selena would be safe from herself here. Will she be safe from them, too?"

"I don't know."

"Is there anything you can do?"

"I don't get involved."

"One more question. Why do they want to destroy Fijora anyway?"

"He tells his followers that Fijora is dangerous, that it's going to rise against them. But that's not his real reason."

"What's his real reason?"

"Fijora has more puppies than any other island."

"His real reason is puppies? But why?"

"Who knows? Maybe he needs lots of little pets…or maybe he's hungry."

\*\*\*

"Come with me," Charlene urged, but Selena shook her head.

"I feel safe here. I think that Aertra was telling the truth. I think Artrea lied to you."

"Aertra kidnapped us! Do you really trust her? And Artrea didn't lie!"

"How do you know? Charlene, I'm not leaving again. Where we run, they run faster. I just can't do it anymore."

\*\*\*

"We had to isolate her. She was a danger to herself and others," Aertra finished. "So, will you help our cause?"

Selena hesitated, thinking of Charlene.

"Selena, it is too late for Charlene. You can't help her now. But you can help us."

\*\*\*

"I have come for you," Artrea said. "But before we leave, I must ask, will you help our cause?"

Charlene hesitated, thinking of Selena.

"Charlene, it's too late for Selena. You can't help her now. But you can help us."

# Deus Ex Machina

*Isabel Canning*

I hear the scratching of trees against trees, a hollowed-out branch locked in never-ending war with chalk-white fibers covered in slivers of blue and red.

I see the darkness creeping into the pulsating red organ that resides in a hollow cage with walls of flesh and bars of bone.

I know the secrets whispered in a hollow tube that forever siphons sound to the lump of neurons that looks and smells of blue cheese but controls our every move.

I am a machine programmed to think and act uniquely toward other machines, all controlled by the quivering organ lodged in our heads, which is kept alive, in turn, by the organ in the chest of bones, muscles, and skin.

I am a human being.

I feel the hardened gray rock beneath my feet as I take in the green and brown colors around me, with round orbs that were implanted in my skull at the beginning of my sorry existence.

I am encased within a globe of green and blue that I walk upon endlessly, never stopping for a moment.

I see tiny machines with simpler minds and different attributes than mine, such as appendages for flight and a clear, melodious call to others of their kind.

I know the way to a large, green box by heart, furnished with necessities, such as food and drink.

I am greeted by two machines. The smaller one shrieks delightedly and embraces the appendages I use for walking.

I live on planet Earth.

The larger machine opens her speaking tube and asks me how the interaction area was, and whether I cranked my speed dial to run.

I find a plate with cut-up meat tubes and tomato paste, and a glass of clear liquid nearby.

I dip the meat into the paste and shovel it into my speaking tube, where it is mashed and sent to the part of my body used for digesting.

I go over to a cushion and use my ocular organs to scan a rectangular object filled with two-dimensional thoughts and ideas.

I live with my mother and sister.

I am on a large cushion covered by smaller cushions. I shut my ocular organs and let the quivering lump in my head take over.

All is quiet in my sleeping compartment. The only sound that remains is the steady beat of the pulsating red organ that resides in the hollow cage with walls of flesh and bars of bone.

I am a human being.

# What a Beautiful Language

# The Confidence Trials:
## A Modern Odyssey (an excerpt)

*Alice Mar-Abe*


Fifteen minutes into lunch, Miranda was surprised to find the corridor leading to the usually bustling art room deserted. It was in the art room that she felt most at ease with herself. Ms. Pythia was always full of spontaneity, an embracer of new ideas and a seeker of substance over form. It mattered more to her that your painting was full of emotion and said what you felt than if it even resembled your original objective.

Miranda tiptoed in. Ms. Pythia whirled from her canvas and blurted out what sounded like, "Noston dizeai meliedea phaidim, Miranda Calida: tov de toi argaleon thesei theos."

Miranda stood there stunned. Strangely, what came to mind was not "Um, come again?" but "What a beautiful language." So that was what she said.

Ms. Pythia smiled. "We think alike."

"What did it mean?"

" 'A sweet, smooth homecoming, renowned Miranda Calida, this is what you seek, but a god will make it hard for you—I know.' "

"A *god*? Did you just say a *god* would make it hard for me?!"

"Oh, no—I meant to say 'a dad.' Though I've no idea whose," she added.

Miranda had known Ms. Pythia to do many strange things, but never to divulge prophecies in ancient languages. A sweet, smooth homecoming?

It was a lucky day when Miranda could still hear peace after her dad came home from work. Even when her parents stayed on different floors, the taut air was tangible. Peace was not the stony silence that carried muted insults on its waves. Peace was serene quiet, dappled with those small details: the coffee machine dripping, the refrigerator humming—even emergency sirens could contribute to peace.

"I think you'll need these," said Ms. Pythia, interrupting Miranda's musings. Miranda gaped down at a pair of orange rubber garden gloves, a sack of grain, a plastic hamster ball, and a set of exquisite paints.

"Right. I'll go put these in my locker," Miranda said politely, backing out of the room.

\*\*\*

Miranda was lying on her bed reading when the garage door rumbled noisily. Footsteps on the stairs. Then Kelly Calida stuck her head into Miranda's room, looking weary. "Hi, honey. How was your day?"

Miranda wanted to laugh and burst into tears. She couldn't begin to explain how bizarre the day had been. When she was running for the bus, the sidewalk beneath her had shot up two stories high, and when she'd impulsively jumped off to escape, she'd landed as lightly as a dandelion seed! A whirring fan swelled to the size of a minivan! She'd been attacked by five querulous chickens and a manic hamster! She'd painted a masterpiece on a disappearing door! But she settled for, "It was good."

"Glad to hear it. Tonight might be another Pizza Hut night; do you mind?"

"Sounds great!" Miranda replied. She'd eat pizza and go to bed. No more of these fantastical events—she felt like that old Greek character, Odysseus, undergoing a series of grueling trials, when both of them were only trying to sail smoothly home!

\* \* \*

It had begun. Miranda could hear thunder and lightning crashing outside the fortress that was her room, but she was beyond caring. The first few times her parents had fought, she'd opened her door a crack and listened concernedly; when it continued, she plugged her ears while fighting back tears. Now, she listened to her iPod and was able to pretend that the yelling was part of someone else's life.

So the prophecy was right! Who cared? Whoever thought her parents' fight would make a difficult final test was so wrong. All she had to do was—**"MIRANDA!"**

A summons? When she composedly entered the kitchen, her father began, "Miranda, is it OKAY with you that your mother puts you in danger by leaving the house unguarded when she FORGETS to shut the garage door after her?"

Miranda's days as a peacemaker were over.

"I am *not* going to take sides," she said.

Miranda was so experienced at putting protective walls around herself that she walked out feeling close to an absence of emotion. At dinner, she nodded and smiled distantly as her parents apologized for their behavior. That might have been the end of it. But as she sat there, munching on her crust, something didn't feel right. She'd conquered the final trial with a cool and rational response, but cool and rational was definitely not how she felt. Miranda hurled the crust roughly onto her plate and slammed her back into her chair.

"Miranda?" her mom asked.

"I'm not at peace in my own home," she said quietly, but she couldn't keep the volcano out of her voice. "I had a terribly trying day, and I come home looking for peace, and I was doing fine until your fighting screwed everything up, like always! And I HATE being the rope in your game of tug-of-war."

She stormed to her room, leaving her parents with stunned, frozen expressions. Once inside, she flung everything out of her dresser, launching each pair of socks at the door with noisy thumps. Tearing the sheets off her bed, she trampled them into a crumpled heap, then she ripped her certificates off the walls.

When she had wreaked utter devastation upon her oh-so-carefully-arranged room, she flopped onto her sheetless mattress and berated herself. She wasn't three; tantrums weren't acceptable. Now she'd failed the most important trial.

Throughout the day, the strange trials had been teaching her to believe in herself. Yet when it counted, she'd lacked that essential mental strength to maintain her wall. The wonderful wall of safety from—Miranda stopped. She was wrong. True, the wall shielded her from the fights. But too often it hid her own emotions from her. It couldn't stay.

She had *needed* this, needed to come to terms with her feelings and be able to express them, to have confidence in how she really felt. Miranda silently thanked whatever deranged deity had created the trials, which had, in the end, freed her. Or had she been the one creating them?

Miranda was ready to find what she sought. This time, with confidence.

# Sunnah's Time Capsule

*Sunnah Rasheed*

Dear person of the future (whenever that future may be):

If you're reading this, then you've found my time capsule. I want to be a bit mysterious, but as you read on, you'll find you know me pretty well. My name is Sunnah…like the sun, and then nah. Not Suna. Not Sauna. Today is August 27, 2009. I'm an eleven-year-old girl about to start sixth grade. I live in Seattle with my sentimental eight-year-old sister, Aalia. We also live with my awesome dad, Nasir (nas – er), and my awesome mom, Shannon.

My dad just discovered he *could* actually be a handyman. Ever since he built Aalia a tree house for her birthday, he has been on a roll, fixing things left and right. My mom is just as awesome as my dad. She's super supportive and is really the perfect mom. There's nothing more to say about her. Not that my dad isn't perfect, he's great, too. My sister is awesome…in her own way.

I have always wanted a dog, but in second grade I was obsessed with cats. I wore cat ears every day. Now I'm more of a dog person, but back then it was all about cats. To teach my sister and me some responsibility, my parents actually got us a cat. Her name is Oreo, and she is the calmest living thing I've ever laid eyes on. After that we got Abbie.

Earlier this year, my dad threw out the idea that he was thinking about getting a dog. This was a shock to everyone. I worked until early June, putting together a bunch of presentations, and turned my dad's fleeting idea into a plan. We found the perfect dog! At least that's what we thought. Actually, she is the spazziest thing. We're working on training, though. She's pretty good...at sitting. Overall, these pets have taught me the many sides of responsibility.

Speaking of teaching, my favorite teacher EVER recently moved away. Mrs. Storms was a highly capable fifth and sixth grade teacher. I'd been looking forward to being in her class since second grade. She wasn't "all that" because she was nice, funny, and occasionally gave us candy. She was amazing because she incorporated humor into her work and gave us the tools to teach ourselves. She made each class enjoyable and fun with exciting projects, and she made me excited for school every day. In a very odd way, she was kind of like Dumbledore from *Harry Potter*. I don't know if I'll ever become a teacher, but if I do, Mrs. Storms inspired me.

Before wrapping this up, I'd like to mention that the environment and economy are failing right now. If that is still going on in your futuristic time—H. E. L. P. Just like every vote counts, every hand does too. The fact that there's enough ozone for you to go outside and find this time capsule is a good sign, though.

I don't know where life will lead me or how the world will change, but I live my life well, and that's all that matters.

Thanks for hearing me out,
Sunnah Rasheed

# Bringing Stacey Home

*Shamile Aldossary*

"Hey Stacey," I called, as she slouched toward me. It was an extraordinarily hot day, and all I wanted to do was hit the beach with Stacey before our big soccer game. As I made my way over to her I couldn't help but feel that today was different, and we wouldn't be going to the beach.

Stacey is what most people would call middle class. She has straight blonde hair and a tan complexion. Her big brown eyes are her most valuable feature, but she always says that she wishes she had my green eyes; she's never satisfied with herself. My family is a bit wealthier. My dad was the inventor of hotel swipe cards, and my mom…well, her name was Margret, and the last time I saw her I was four, and she was boarding her last plane ride. Today my big chocolate-colored curls rest on top of my summer tan that Stacey and I have been working on together. We will both be fifteen in four months, though I'll turn fifteen exactly two days and seven hours before her. In spite of our differences, we are extremely close. We could even pass for sisters.

"Stacey, is something wrong?" I asked. Her eyes looked as if she hadn't slept in days, and it felt like five minutes had passed before she gave me an answer.

"Huh," she said, as though she wasn't even listening to me.

"Are you okay?"

"Yeah, totally. I'm fine. Don't worry. Why? Does it look like something's wrong?" she added with a friendly chuckle and a guilty look on her face.

"Hmmm," I muttered with curiosity.

Stacey reached for her phone as it vibrated to the tune of "Who Let the Dogs Out." After a minute she got off the phone and started walking away. "Well, I got to go eat dinner," she said. "I'll see you later, Jocey."

"Bye…loves ya!" I called. I looked at my phone to see that it was only 4:45—a little too early for even an early dinner.

\*\*\*

That night I jumped into my orange and pink polka-dotted bed. I slipped off my shorts and the swimsuit I didn't even get to use at the beach with Stacey, and I pulled on a pink tank top and silky purple pajama bottoms. I hoped Stacey would act a little more like herself in time for our big soccer game against California the next day. We had played soccer together our whole lives, and it was the sport we couldn't live without. There's something about the way the wind brushes through my hair when I'm sprinting down the field, and the way I smack my feet against the ball with all my might, straight into the goal. Our team is the National U-14 soccer team of Florida, and if we beat California, we would only have Washington and Virginia between us and the National Championship. I totally couldn't wait, and I hoped Stacey was just as ready as I was!

The tune from *That 60's Show* started blaring from under my pillow, and I reached for my neon orange iPhone. I rolled over and answered. "Hey, Stace! Hope you're feeling better, because we are kicking major butt tomorrow!"

"Um, Jocey, about that. I can't come to the game tomorrow."

"What? Ha-ha, very funny."

"No, really."

"What the heck! Why?" I screamed into my phone.

"I'm...I'm sick." She sneezed. "Sorry...bye."

Stacey immediately hung up. My mouth and my mind were left wide open as I wondered what was going to happen at the game without Stacey—and more importantly, what was going on with Stacey. As I lay in bed I couldn't stop thinking about everything. I popped two Sickvil PMs in my mouth and rolled over onto my side. I needed to get some sleep and concentrate on the game tomorrow.

\* \* \*

My mouth was a straight line as I got out of the soccer van.

"Come on Black, cheer up! Remember: it's all right, it's okay, we will kick their butts today!" Marcy sang to try to make me smile. "We all want Stacey to be here—you know that! Now turn that frown upside down. We're Cheetahs!"

"Humph," I huffed. I marched over to the white soccer nets and practiced my leg stretches. I lay down on the grass and checked out my new pink and neon green jersey. I couldn't get Stacey's voice from last night out of my head.

The ref blew his whistle, and everyone ran towards the middle of the field. The other team was wearing yellow-and-black striped jerseys with "The Wasps" written across their chests. The day had started off bad enough, and now we had an intimidating team to play against. We all got into our positions and the game began.

I couldn't believe how well I was playing. I think the fact that Stacey had let me down made me want to win even more. Number fourteen was guarding me, and I barely managed to juggle the ball to Margo. Number fourteen was about double my height with big curly red hair, and after I passed her I felt like I could take on anyone.

The game ended, and we won 6-3. I called Stacey afterwards to tell her how well we had played and that we would be moving on in the championships, but her mom picked up and said she had gone out for a java smoothie. What had gotten into that girl, I wondered. But I didn't even have a chance to be mad because I immediately got a feeling—a feeling that was almost impossible to describe in my gut that made my heart beat ten times faster.

\* \* \*

Our family driver, Rob, dropped me off at Write Beach Library. As I played the role of Nancy Drew, I craved something good to drink. I walked two blocks down to Moonbucks and ordered my regular hot drink, a caramel frap with no whip. As I called Rob to come get me, I glanced at the tree that shaded a little bench outside the café and saw Stacey.

"Stacey!" I yelled. "Come here!"

Without even turning around to see where I was, Stacey stuffed a hand in her pocket and sprinted away. I wanted to go run after her, but a strange feeling held me back— the same feeling as the night before. After Stacey had disappeared I circled the beach with my coffee in one hand and a ton of questions in the other. I found a decent shaded spot under the trees to sit down and browsed through the books I had checked out. *The Difference between Puberty and Changing* was the first one. This is pretty silly, I thought to myself. Was I taking this too far? I opened the second book, called *Lost*. It had several different stories written by teenagers about people that they loved either dying or leaving. I read the book until I went back to the library, where Rob picked me up. Sitting in our silver stretch Cadillac, I couldn't even put a finger on what I was thinking.

At home I lay down in my orange-and-pink striped hammock and studied the rest of the books. "Tonight," I said to myself, "I will find out what's been going on." My head buzzed with thoughts about Stacey and her mystery problem. What puzzled me the most was why she couldn't even tell me. What would be so private, so embarrassing, that she couldn't tell me? I was the only person in her life that she told everything to—from the time her dad moved out to the day in the fifth grade she found a wallet and didn't return it. There was nothing we kept from each other.

I was determined to know what was going on in her mind, so I made a list of possibilities.

1. She was feeling randomly depressed.
2. She misses her dad.
3. Someone died.
4. Ugh, maybe she just doesn't like me anymore.

I immediately slid my blue denim shorts over my bright blue and white Boston Eagle bathing suit, grabbed a blueberry muffin, and headed out the door and down the courtyard towards Stacey's house. Once I was there I went to the nearest pay phone, near the public tennis court, and dialed Stacey's number. There was a sick feeling inside me that came from knowing I wouldn't get an answer if I used my own cell phone. It made me feel sad, and my heart sunk down in my stomach.

"Hello?" Stacey answered.

Without time to feel more sympathy, I replied, "I'm at your house. Open the door."

"What? Why?"

"Open it, or I'm coming in."

"Fine. I'll be down in a sec!"

As I walked up to the white door of Stacey's brown, two-story house, I could hear her stomping down the stairs, followed by a dramatic opening of the door. "Hey, what's up?" Stacey asked as if everything was back to normal.

"Let's go to the beach," I said.

"Sure," Stacey said. She looked like she had no intention of leaving her house, but that she also didn't want to disappoint me even more. We walked side by side the two blocks to Tontu Beach, small-talking. I wasn't sure how I was supposed to bring up the list I had made. The weather was warm—not too hot, but warm enough to make you want to take your clothes off. But Stacey didn't even bring a suit. She just sat there and played with the sand in her hands.

"What's with you these days, Stace?" I asked as I wrote my name in the sand with a big stick I had found.

"What are you talking about? Geez, Jocey, you really need to chill out!" The tone of her voice made me certain that everything wasn't okay, and that she knew exactly what I was talking about.

"I was just asking…talk to your dad lately?"

"I haven't spoken to him since he left five years ago. You know that."

"Yeah, I know. Just making sure it wasn't that."

"What wasn't that? Nothing's wrong, okay? Now, I have to go before my mom gets home from the store." She got up angrily but looked me in the eye with so much remorse that I knew I needed to do something. Grabbing her tote and stumbling in the sand, Stacey was gone faster than I could say goodbye.

* * *

Well, I guessed I could go ahead and check numbers two

and three off my list. I tossed and turned between the sheets of my queen-sized bed, trying to sleep. I couldn't get Stacey out of my mind. I knew what she was doing now, but I had no idea why she was doing it. Something in me felt like I should try to talk to her again, but when my mouth opened no words would come out. I'd never had to deal with anything like this before.

By morning I knew exactly what I had to do. I jumped off my bed and got ready for the day. First I picked out my blue denim shorts and a red and pink tank top that Stacey bought me last summer; she has the same one in orange and yellow. As my normal routine continued, I added one element: an extremely important phone call.

It was the day of our last championship game against the Virginia Wolverines, but I'd chosen not to go. There were more important things on my to-do list. I hopped onto my turquoise Vespa and drove around the pier six times to kill fifteen minutes and to prepare myself for what would happen in the near future. Was it just me, or was something extremely scary going to happen? I'd always had a way of knowing what types of emotions were going to come next. My dad called it my special power. I knew that I wasn't going to be able to sleep soundly that night.

When I reached Stacey's, I gave the door two solid knocks. The door quickly swung open.

"Hello, Jocey," said Ms. Collin, Stacey's mom. "I've been waiting for you."

"Sorry, I couldn't find Rob."

"Oh, right." There was an awkward pause.

"Anyways, Stacey's up in her room."

"Okay," I said.

With excitement and complete nervousness hiding under my tone, I headed up the narrow stairway behind Ms. Collin toward Stacey's shut door. I held onto the wooden railing with my right hand and the brochure in my left.

This was probably the millionth time I'd been over to this house, and would probably be the first time that Stacey and I wouldn't be sharing any laughs.

Stacey's mom blasted open the door to find Stacey sitting on the floor against her desk with a whatever look in her eyes. I gasped, but my eyes stayed wide open. Everything I pictured couldn't come close to how terrible this was. I looked into her eyes until she finally said something.

"What?" Stacey barked.

I could see the fear that Ms. Collin had for her daughter. Something had just happened that she would never have wanted to accept, something that no one would ever forget, something that she thought only happened in movies. It was this moment that scared her the most. Her eyes swelled up, her body started shaking, and within seconds Ms. Collin ran out of the room crying hysterically. What mother wants to walk into her daughter's room to see her angel sniffing lines of white powder off her desk where she once worked on her homework?

Tears slid from my eyes while I stood there wondering what would happen next. I would like to say that I already knew, that I did have a special power, but at that moment I felt as lost as Stacey was.

"Why?" I asked with a disgusted tone.

"Why what? Why am I doing this? Or why couldn't I tell you earlier?"

"Why all of it! Why start snorting cocaine, or God knows what other crap has been up your nose!"

Stacey took a heavy breath, stood up, and burst into

tears as she fell face-first onto her bed. I headed over to the purple bedspread and sat next to Stacey's crying body. I sat there until her tears stopped and she could breathe normally again. She got up to look at me and whispered something I couldn't make out. I knew she was trying to apologize to me. I slid my left hand into hers and handed her the brochure from the clinic that I picked up before heading to her house.

Before she could even look at what I handed her, Stacey gave me a huge hug. At that moment I couldn't help but feel incredibly sorry for her. I walked her down the stairs into the kitchen where she gave her mom a hug. There were still tears running down Ms. Collin's face that melded into Stacey's. My eyes were as red as tomatoes, and I just wanted to go back to the beach with Stacey and finish the tan contest we started in our ninth grade year, and see what else came our way from there. I just wanted my sister back.

Stacey turned away from her mom and looked at me.

"Our final game is today. Why aren't you there?"

"Well, something more important came up," I said with a grin.

"I think we can still make it if my mom drives us," Stacey said.

Everything felt so right, but I knew that even if Stacey and I went to the game and won, she still had a problem that I wished she would deal with.

I guess it's important to know that I played really well at our last game. It was good to play soccer with my best friend cheering me on. It was amazing to win the trophy our team had worked so hard to get, but even better knowing that Stacey would be all right, and that I didn't lose the game, or her.

\*\*\*

Four weeks later, Ms. Collin and I drive to the hospital in her green Honda, but this time we don't have to park. This time Stacey is waiting outside. We're definitely going to the beach. I've gotten three shades lighter since Stacey left, and Stacey...yeah, let's not even start. Since she's been here it looks like she hasn't even been outside. It's good to know that once we drive away from this place we will never have to make the trip back.

"Let's dive in Joce."

I put a smile on my face as we stand down on the ocean dock. All the horrors of the past month have disappeared. I got my best friend back, I got my sister back, and now we can finally finish what we started. I grab her from behind on the backside, and we cannonball into our summer paradise.

# Bubba

*Rammah Elbasheer*

It was 12:05 when the police came. They knocked on the door quietly. I was in my room waiting for Mom and Dad to come back. They were supposed to be here three hours ago, so I rushed to the door, but all I saw was the policeman with his head low and his cap in his hands. "Oh God," I mumbled.

Next thing I knew, I was at the police station being told about my parents' death. They were killed in a plane crash. Police suspect Russian terrorists caused it because last month there were two crashes just like it. Anyway, no one survived the crash except for the terrorists who knocked out the pilots and steered the plane downward before parachuting off. Later they found out the pilots got hit in the head with fire extinguishers. After being told all this, it was like someone hit me with a fire extinguisher. I couldn't believe it. *How'd this happen? Didn't anyone see the terrorists?* I was confused. I asked the policeman, "No one survived? Are you sure? Maybe they're just unconscious."

"Nope, they're all dead. A lot of kitchen supplies and metal flew around when they crashed," the policeman said. "It's impossible for them to be alive."

"I'm going home to sleep," I said while walking toward the door.

"Hey, by the way, in a week a caseworker is coming to find

you a foster home," the policeman said on my way out. I pretended I didn't hear him. On the way home I thought about all this. *A caseworker? A new home? Do the police even care my parents are dead?*

Then suddenly, two rough hands grabbed my shoulders and pulled me back. Before I could yell, another pair of hands held my mouth and put a piece of oddly scented cloth on my nose . . . suddenly I felt so drowsy . . . I wanted to sleep. So, while the men tied me up and led me to a black car with heavily tinted windows, I closed my eyes. Right before I fell asleep I realized three things: *one, I've been drugged; two, I'm being kidnapped; three, somehow, my arm is bleeding.*

When I woke up, I was in a green room tied to a chair with drool all over my pants. I heard bits of a conversation in the other room. They were saying something about my parents. I got excited. *Maybe they know something about my parents!* I wanted to jump up and down. In fact I tried, but the rope stopped me and sent the chair hurling toward the floor, my body of course flying with it. I noticed a Hello Kitty bandage on my arm where I was bleeding earlier. I laughed, and then my head hit the floor, knocking me unconscious. . . When I got up again, I saw two men. One came up to me and said, "Your parents are dead, hmmm?"

I looked up. By his voice I could tell they were Russian. Unsteadily, I said, "Ya, they're dead."

"It's not our fault, you know, we just wanted to kill George bin Laddin," the other said.

"George bin Laddin?"

"Your father . . ." the first said.

"What!?" I said, alarmed.

". . . isn't your father's name George Lad?"

"Yeah…" I said carefully.

"Well, *Lad* stands for *Laddin*."

"Okay." (I didn't care much anymore, I just wanted to die.)

"Well, I thought you should know."

"Hmmm... whatever—I wanna die."

"Are you sure?"

"Yeah," I said.

Suddenly, I heard a loud crack echo through the room, and I had pain all over my chest.

"You killed him!"one of the men said irritably.

"He said he wanted to die . . . I ended his misery."

"Whatever."

They started to leave . . . and I died.

Then I heard a faint voice ."Bubba! Bubba!"the voice said. I opened my eyes and I saw my parents. It was all a dream! "Hey Mom, Hey Dad, you're ALIVE!"

"What?" they said, startled.

"Never mind," I said, and I got ready for school and went outside to catch the school bus.

# Knowing

*Kyrie Scarce*

You know things. Things you shouldn't know. But once you know something it's impossible to un-know it, and anyway maybe you don't *want* to un-know something just because it's dangerous. It smacks of adventure, now that you think about it, and who doesn't like a good adventure story?

Besides, it's not going to get *really* dangerous until someone knows you know. This school's got some good psychics, but you have a mental defense that'll be tricky to undermine. Not completely solid, but tricky. They won't know you know something for awhile, and even if they *do*, it'll take a good chunk of time to figure out just *what* it is you know.

So.

You know things. Things that might lead you to have a grand old time escaping. You'll flee laser beams and dodge cops and slink past Wanted posters with your face on them, sever all your old ties—all while searching for a place where they'll never, ever find you…

But you shouldn't visualize that. Someone might notice. And then they'll know you know something.

# Salt Water was Mixing in with Brook Water

# The Boy at Bubble Brook

*Zoë Rogan*

Brushing dirt off a formerly blue dress, I stood up and began climbing on piles of broken glass and tires. My hem caught on a piece of bottle at its sharpest point. I felt a sting on my leg and looked down to see a cut with a stream of blood rushing down. I stumbled off the trash-heap, getting more scratches, and limped over to Bubble Brook to wash off the blood. Little did I know the brook was mixed with salt water. My cut stung, and I took my leg out immediately. The water hadn't helped.

Then you marched down in a neat and tidy sailor suit. You stopped behind me and shoved me into the lake. Every scrape on my body stung, but you didn't know about my cuts. When you saw blood-red water, you pulled me up and took out a bandage.

At twelve, you confessed on Bubble Brook's little wooden bridge that you didn't have a clue how to swim and you were too scared to try. You explained that your uncle had tried to teach your older brother how to swim when he six. Your brother hit his skull on a pointed stone, suffered amnesia, and was still in the hospital. After you finished telling me the story, a passing boy picked up your wiry body and threw you into the brook. I dove in and rescued you, but you never thanked me.

At twenty-two, you proposed and preparations were made.

Three years after the wedding, I walked with you on a beach. A kidnapper grabbed you from behind and pulled you back. Winds whispered to me to fight for you, but when I finally lunged, he was gone. And so were you.

Now I wish that you were alive, and by my side. There is no more booming laugh, delicious cooking, kind words. No more you. All the life is taken out of me. My good life is finished.

## So You Think You Can Tell Heaven from Hell

*Fate Syewoangnuan*

Another rainy day. Another cloudy, colorless, murky day. In this town you either freeze to death or get fried, depending on the day. On the two nice days each year you get to see the beautifully polluted sky. That's why the best place to be here is either underground or dead. Well, maybe asleep. But the point is, stay in this town long enough and you'll get to enjoy sleeping…forever.

Somewhere in time, humanity ended up getting so screwed up that emotion became a bad thing. Here you go to work, come back, and sleep. Up in that big, fancy palace in the sky was the government, up in the last good place the world knew.

What do I do? Survive. My only goal in life is to make sure I still have one. If I wake up the next day still breathing, I have done my job. A rebel is actually the best thing to be— free from any chains. You can do whatever—they gave up on having police a long time ago. I've decided that's what I have to do: be a rebel.

On one of those freezing, foggy days, I was dashing through the icy wasteland. Well, it was a city, but all the color had faded long ago. The snow covered the ground, shimmering in the blazing sun. How weird—it was about ninety degrees, but a fog was freezing over everything it touched. I ignored this and decided dying in this weather would be even weirder. But then I came upon a wall. Just a solid, white wall. The only thing weird about it was it was completely immaculate except for a single brick in the wall. It was a very tall and wide wall, connected to two others pointing in the same direction. I slowly approached the brick and tapped on it. Suddenly, the whole wall was gone but the brick remained, floating there in space. Before I could take a closer look, I noticed a very large tranquilizer dart poking into my shoulder. The world began to spin, darkness clouded my eyes, and I was being dragged across the cold, icy ground....

My eyes slowly opened and for an instant light flooded in. Soon, shapes and colors began to return. I wished my eyes were still closed. I found myself staring down the barrel of a gun. Looming behind was a seven-foot-tall brute with muscles wider than my own torso. His cold, bloodshot eyes seemed to drill into my head.

"Who are you?" I groaned with a scratchy voice box.

"The real question is, who are you?" he bellowed.

"My name is Ando Takensei. I'm a nothing, a nobody, so you have absolutely no reason to keep me here."

"If you're really not government scum, then burn this." He handed me a lighter and the government symbol on a flag. "But if you make any funny moves, then I'll give you a one-way ticket to hell!"

"Trust me, I'm already there," I muttered, holding the lighter to the flag. Here, if you work for the government, burning the authentic sign would actually be like immolating yourself. Since I was very much not on fire, the brute unshackled me...and then bagged my head.

"Until we can fully trust you, you must not know the

way to our base," he said, and began dragging me for what seemed to be hours.

Finally, even after my feet were scarred and bloodied, we stopped. The hood was ripped off of my head and standing in front of me was a five-foot-tall man. Abruptly, he asked, "Do you know how to use this?" and pointed to a shiny pistol.

"Yes."

He tossed it to me and said, "Then you're in. Get some rest. At noon tomorrow we strike."

I walked through the cold, metallic halls and opened the door to a small room. I really wish I knew who "we" was, But since they obviously didn't like the government, I could probably trust them. My muscles ached tremendously and I lowered myself into the bed and closed my eyes...

\* \* \*

Childhood was rough. I grew up watching the most beautiful of cities and landscapes slowly decay under a sickening environment. I woke up one day and my whole family was gone. I didn't know where they had gone or why, There was nothing that would help me pursue them, so I never did. I spent half my life in hiding—as a second child, I had an automatic death sentence. So I ran and I hid, time and time again. You keep moving, you don't look back, and that's what keeps you alive. Never stay in one place too long. I've run all the way from New York to Washington state. That's when they decided to switch to a dictatorship, a crushing blow after humanity had finally been united. I wasn't the best of people. I had to steal for a living. Living alone can make you more confused than you'd ever dreamed of being. But really, I dream it every night...

I jolted awake as an icy cold bucket of water splashed over my head. "Get up." The short man said, and I half dragged myself to follow him. We walked through a seemingly never-ending maze of doors and halls until we came to a table. I heard the door click and lock behind me, and we both sat down at a table in the center of the room. He told me, "Look, I owe you an explanation. We are the rebels. The only reason you are here now is that you somehow managed to find our secret base, and we can't have you ratting us out. But since we hardly know you, we can afford to lose you, and that is why YOU are being sent to do one of our very dangerous yet important missions." This was not a very comforting thought. "For years we have fought against the government, and for years we have failed to truly DO anything. But now we have a plan...."

An appalling darkness spread across the landscape. The forest floor was wet from the melted snow. Through the leaves, moonbeams struggled to cast light on the sullen earth. Through a mildly purple haze I could see the outline of the building. The shadows of my allies were flanking me. The soft crunching of our footsteps on the fallen leaves made us nervous. If we failed, the Earth would spend many more years like this, a sad excuse for a planet. I had nothing left to fight for, so I was fighting for what's right for the first time in my life. The feeling was not as comforting as I would've hoped.

The red light flashed and I stopped. A small number of shadows disappeared, followed by a series of thuds.

The green light flashed and the coast was clear.

I sprinted across the clearing until I saw a wall. The others knelt besides me and one cut open a hole in a small grate in the wall. I climbed in and started crawling through, this time no one followed. The steel against my skin was making me more nervous; this could be the last thing I ever did. This building was the final barrier to invade the thing that made our world like this, so it must be destroyed. The sheer intensity of it all was rattling my skull.

I found the room where I had been instructed to place the bomb. I quickly unscrewed the gate and as silently as possible laid it down on the floor. I estimated the center of the room and placed the bomb there. I armed it, and then began to run toward the grate when I heard footsteps. A man was whispering in a low voice to his group.

"They don't think we know they're here. It'll be a complete massacre! They'll never know what hit them…"

I realized what he was saying and knew he was right. During an ambush there's no way they'd make it out alive. What should I do? Wait a second…they don't know about the bomb… There's no time! I thought. I have to stay here and fight them off, or else the other rebels will die. If the rebels die, then the last shred of hope dies with them. The only way they can make it out is if I hold the agents off them. One thing's for certain: I have to be here when that bomb explodes.

I fired a salvo of bullets at the onrushing squadron. They fell. Fire began to break out. The building was collapsing. I covered my mouth to shield it from the smoke.

I ran into the government agents. Hundreds of them were rushing to the exit. The ticking of the bomb began to quicken. I took a rock and hurled it at the door control.

"You mad man! We will ALL die in here!"

"I know."

I had a lot of regrets. I did some bad things and if I could, I would've done things differently. But at this point I had nothing left to lose. If dying in here would give the people a better shot at life, then I would proudly do so.

The walls exploded, leaving only a titanium-enforced one, and a cloud of smoke and flames began to swallow up the halls. For some reason, for that instant before my body was incinerated, I smiled.

# The Round House

*Oscar White*

As I walked down the street, I came to a old broken-down wooden sign. It said: beware of the round house. I said to myself, there's no such thing, and that's when I saw it. It was wide and round and as big as a mansion. Suddenly, the door swung open and I watched in horror as a ghost floated out. It was a white mist and screaming without a mouth. It came towards me. I thought, what am I going to do now?!

What should I do? Run around it into the house? Well, I should give it a try. I ran around it, then looked back. It wasn't following me. So I ran into the house. The air was stiff and dusty, the light was dim and weak. I saw entrances to the upstairs, basement, and back yard. I took a deep breath and started climbing the stairs. I finally got upstairs and looked around. I saw five rooms. I walked over to one of the doors and knocked. No answer. I pushed open the door. Suddenly, there was a loud scream—the same as the one from the ghost. A shadow darted across the wall. Then everything went black.

I kept hearing someone say my name, but I was still asleep. I decided to wake up. So I did. A kid was standing over me. I looked around. I was in a yard, lying on grass. I jumped up and started to talk, but he shushed me.

"You are in the garden of zombies."

I laughed. He looked surprised.

"There is no such thing," I said.

Suddenly, I saw people coming out from behind stuff. They looked like normal people, but there was only one thing strange: they were all blank-eyed. Oh! It's a trap! They were getting closer. Then, out of nowhere, there was a blinding light. When it went away the zombies were gone, and I was in my bed. I got up. I noticed a note on my desk, written in red ink:

"We'll come back soon, and then we'll get you."

# Grandma's Special Soup

*Maggie Grasseschi*

"Billy!" Mom was scary when she was angry. "Eat your lunch."

"Shan't!" Billy sang, swinging his legs. "Don't like soup."

She tried the guilt trip. "Billy, your grandmother made it just for you."

Billy wasn't having it. "Shan't!" he sang again. "Hasn't got goldfish in it!"

Mom sighed and poured some goldfish in Billy's soup. "Now?"

"Shan't!" Billy sang again.

It continued this way until the tomato soup that was Billy's lunch was covered in goldfish, cheese, pretzels and frosting. Still, Billy wouldn't eat.

"Shan't, shan't, shan't, shan't, shan't!"

Finally, the soup was topped with whipped cream and chocolate.

I woke up with a start.

That was the last time I ate Grandma's Special Soup before bed.

# Atlantis Reborn
# (an excerpt)

*Josh Abrahamson*

"Attention!" Lieutenant James Harris bellowed the command. Admiral Ronald Anderson, the commanding officer aboard the USS Titan, strode out in front of us.

There were thirty of us all together, lined up along the deck in full uniform. We were an elite group of marines known as the 73rd Armored Division, founded by President Obama in 2009. We were in charge of carrying out the most dangerous missions of the U.S. Navy. I was the team leader, Staff Sergeant Casius Hanes. The admiral had brought us here for a special briefing on our latest mission.

"As you all know," the graying admiral stated, "the last two years have been a mess for us and our allies. Terrorism, starting with Al Quaeda and now Hydra and Draco, has soared. Just last week Draco blew the torch off the Statue of Liberty in New York. We do not have the kind of power, nor enough energy resources, to solve this worldwide problem.

"Fortunately, we have some hope. An associate of mine, Commander Bill Enderby, captain of the USS Small Fry, has found an alternative power source on a small, uncharted island in the South Atlantic. It is our job to secure this power source."

"It is very old, according to Commander Enderby," added Lt. Harris.

"With all due respect, Sir," interrupted one of the soldiers, "why do we need armed forces to secure this object?"

"Because Hydra and Draco have always been one step ahead of us," replied the admiral, "and we suspect they know about this source. Hydra may in fact be on the way now to secure it, and I do not want to miss an opportunity to obtain an upper hand. Understand?"

"Yes, Sir."

"Now, an ally in England has agreed to give us any assistance necessary," the admiral continued. "In exactly four hours, a naval transport ship and an air cargo plane are going to meet us and Commander Enderby at the rendezvous point. I need four of you to make room in the hold for the equipment being dropped off."

I was one of the ones chosen to make room in the hold, and proceeded to the belly of the ship.

\*\*\*

After we'd finished with the hold, I was called to the conference room. The admiral and Lt. Harris were waiting for me.

"Sit down, Sergeant," said the admiral firmly.

"Sir?" I asked.

"We need to show you something."

"As you know," began Lt. Harris, "Hydra is perhaps the most advanced terrorist organization we have ever seen. They have weapons that can destroy steel in seconds, not to mention human flesh."

"What would you like me to do?" I asked.

"Not just you," said the admiral, "Your entire team."

He picked up a remote control and pressed a button. The screen on the back wall rotated to reveal a suit — not a business suit but a cross between a spacesuit and a robot. Dark black in color, it resembled something out of a Star Wars film. A containment unit on the back was connected to various parts of the suit by three hoses. Two of them were for oxygen. The other one attached to what looked like a propane torch on the left arm, in place of the hand. The faceplate was mirrored, reflecting the sunlight, and it was sealed to prevent gas and dust from coming in. A contraption at the base of the helmet resembled an air filter. The right arm was attached to the barrel of a Gatling-style mini-gun, again in place of the hand.

"These are the new suits for your armored division." said the admiral. "The gun on the right can be replaced with a grenade or rocket launcher, and the torch at the end of the left arm has a dual function flame and nerve gas nozzle. If the need arises, there's a switch that folds the guns back to let gloves fall into place. Well?"

"Uh…," I said, my mouth slack.

"We figured that if Hydra was going to hit us with their full arsenal, then we would be ready. This suit has been sitting in the testing room since 2010."

"Um…thank you, Sir."

"You're welcome, Sergeant. Now, the suits also have an advanced steel plating made of timantium, a mixture of admantium and titanium steel. You would have to be hit directly in a weak point by something incredibly powerful to be killed. The metal has also had micro-sensor wiring technology embedded in its surface. It's laser-sensitive, so if a sniper's got a scope on you, an alarm will go off in the helmet. Figured that it might come in handy."

"When we get to the rendezvous point, we'll test these suits," said Lt. Harris.

\*\*\*

The first three hours of the mission were hell.

First, Hydra intercepted the Titan and destroyed it, forcing us to be rescued. Second, the supply ship and cargo plane were late meeting the ship that rescued us, coincidentally, the USS Small Fry. (Commander Enderby had radioed them, told them to meet us at the island, and gave them the coordinates.) And, third, I had to share a bunk with a young recruit who wouldn't stop blabbering on about the battle.

The supply plane delivered weapons, each with its own crate of extra ammunition. Good thing, too, because most of ours were lost in the explosion of the Titan. The only thing salvaged was the admiral's custom mini-gun which he called "Old Faithful." It shot thirty shotgun shells full of birdshot in less than a minute.

All thirty of us in the division received our specialized suits. Two of my men had unique arm attachments. Riker, my second in command, had a rocket launcher, and a young recruit named Benjamin had a sniper rifle.

After traveling into the forest of the island, the team, along with Admiral Anderson, met Dr. Meredith Jansen, a British archeologist who had arrived on the island via the supply plane.

"The source is a most unusual artifact," she told us, as we began hiking deeper into the forest. "It dates to somewhere around 1500 BC, but still produces energy. It's also quite small, so it may not be enough power for you.

"I must admit, Sir," she said, turning her attention to me, "That suit makes you look very sexy."

I stopped abruptly and whipped my head up, striking a branch as I did so.

"Clang!!" went the suit.

"Oof!" I exclaimed and tumbled down a small slope, destroying the vegetation along the way. Everyone laughed.

"Ah, here we are," announced Jansen.

It was a square clearing, roughly thirty feet in either direction. In the center was a stone column, and at the top of the column was a small box-like structure, about two feet long and a foot wide. It had a hole in the top and a small cylinder in its side that would occasionally pulse with a glowing blue light, brighter, then dimmer.

"The outside is made of a rubber-like substance that blocks energy from escaping except through this," said Jansen, pointing to the cylinder. "Any raw substance can be fed through the hole and recycled back out through the cylinder into energy."

As she was talking, I looked at the column. It seemed to be made out of a solid piece of stone, but when I tapped it, it was hollow. I looked at the base of the structure and found a depression in the shape of something familiar. I knew what it was.

"Dr. Jansen," I asked, pointing at the box, "May I...?"

"Go on."

I took the box down from the column and fit it into the depression. Then I took out several bullet casings and put them in the hole at the top. All hell broke loose.

The thing started pulsing repeatedly, flashing so fast that it resembled solid blue light. A crackling sound came from it, echoing around the forest. The rest of the crew stared in awed silence.

Suddenly, the ground beneath us erupted, sending us flying and reeling all over the place. A door at the edge of the clearing opened to reveal a yawning cavern, only a bit smaller than the clearing itself. The opening was shaped like two connected semi-circles standing on end.

"What in bloody hell was that?" screamed a disheveled Dr. Jansen from behind a bush.

"The source was a key," I stated. "I figured that out by studying the column for a bit. It was hollow, made of cleverly disguised metal, and there was a depression the exact same shape as the box.

"I also figured that, if the box were a key, then larger power generators might lie behind the opening."

"Terrific deducing, Staff Sergeant!" boomed the admiral. "Let's move on."

I led the way through the cavern, which was actually a long tunnel heading downward. After about an hour, I realized that we had come very far underground, because the rock under our feet was solidified lava, and there was salt water on the cavern walls. I knew we were under the ocean.

After another hour, we could see a light at the end of the tunnel. It looked like sunlight, but it couldn't be, because we hadn't climbed higher.

Continuing on, we emerged into a monstrous cavern. A moving ball of pulsing light lit the cavern like an artificial sun.

From where we were standing, we could see the lake of lava at the bottom of the chamber and a land mass rising out of the center, complete with mountains and lakes of its own. And in the far distance, there was a cluster of structures. I tuned the vision scope of my mask and saw a massive walled city that brought to mind a legend I'd studied in high school.

"Doctor," I asked, "What do you know about Atlantis?"

"It was an ancient but advanced city that was sunk beneath the sea," she said. Realization dawned on her face. "My God! You don't think…"

"Yes. I...I think that we've found it."

Just as the words came out of my mouth, a group of armor-clad beings jumped us from above. They pointed their weapons, sizzling with energy, at us.

"Put your weapons down, men," ordered the admiral. "Pardon the pun, but they got the jump on us."

We were taken to the city. The buildings were unlike any I'd ever laid eyes on, all very tall and built like towers, a massive chessboard full of intricate rooks.

The warriors escorted us to the palace and up to the throne room. The ruler of Atlantis, a wizened old man with dark skin, looked down over us and began to speak.

"Hábla Espanol? Parlez-vous Français? Speak English?"

At the sound of English, we nodded.

"Very well then," he continued. "I am Emperor Sonores, ruler of Atlantis. Why have you come here?"

"With all due respect, Sire," said Dr. Jansen, "the world above is in danger of being taken over by evil. We are..."

"Let me guess. You have come to find a power source that will enable you to overcome this evil?"

"Yes. How did you know that?"

"Many people have come down from the overworld. There are many entrances to Atlantis. You may know an Amelia Earhart?"

"The famed pilot who disappeared in the Pacific Ocean?" asked Lt. James.

"I do not know this Pacific of which you speak," the emperor replied, "but she came through a back entrance to Atlantis and found it so amazing that she spent the rest of her life here. Her grave is on the far side of the city.

"As for the power source, I hear tell of what is happening to the overworld from time to time, from those who have been here and know how to contact me. You cannot have it."

"But, Your Majesty," I sputtered, "without this power source, our people will have to succumb to the will of our enemies."

"You wrong me, Automaton," the emperor said, not understanding that a biological being was inside the armored body. "If we could liberate some of our power we would."

"What is this power source, anyway?" asked the admiral.

"The power comes from several stones," said the emperor. "They rest in the sides of our cavern and are harvested by our great lighthouse in the city of Aneas. The power is then transferred in brilliant wings of light to Duracrist, a crystal that holds all the power in Atlantis.

"Alas, when Atlantis sank beneath the ocean, the old city was destroyed and the Duracrist was lost. We were limited by our remaining energy and so were forced to make machines that could renew it. We cannot liberate any for other purposes, for we have just enough for our own renewal efforts."

"What if we were to locate this Duracrist crystal?" asked Commander Enderby.

"Locate it?" said the emperor incredulously. "I've sent my best hunters and searchers to find the Duracrist, and you think you can find it and bring it back?"

"Sire," said Dr. Jansen, "you may have weaponry and machines that are more advanced than ours, but our searching equipment is more advanced than your hunters' eyes. We could find this Duracrist and bring it to you in return for the power source we seek."

"If you are to go, you are not to go alone. I will send some of my warriors with you."

"Yes, Your Majesty," said the admiral.

*To be continued ...*

# A Potent Enough Curse in a Long-Forgotten French Dialect

## This Is Just to Say

*Lucia Minahan*

This is just to say

I have bitten my little
sister's hand while she
was sleeping.

Which might not have
been the right thing
to do.

Forgive me, it just looked
so tender and sweet just like
a piece of meat.

# Who's the Outlaw?

*Yomna Anan*

"Watch out!" Honk, honk!!

Sorry!" I yell in a very angry voice.

It's 10:30 a.m. I'm gonna be late. Then I remember: late for what? Oh well.

I finally arrive home, and I see my grandparents standing right in front of me. "Uh oh," I think, "I'm busted. Big time!"

"Loui Outlaw! Where were you?!"

"Leave me alone you big idiots!" I yell.

Gasp!!

"Go to your room, Loui!!"

So. . .I go to my room, annoyed, and that's when it happened. I became an outlaw.

Next day, I woke up, and just went to school. As I walked through the hallway, everyone ran away. That's what I thought. I don't know why. People are always avoiding me. Come on! I'm seventeen, and it's about time I find a friend.

It's chemistry now, which I totally fail at. My teacher, Ms. Ticks, says we are doing a project, but we need a partner. Of course I'm not gonna get one. So, I go up to Ms. Ticks and say, "Yo! I don't feel like doing this stupid project of yours, so I'm not gonna do it! Later, Grandma!"

"Mr. Outlaw, please come back here immediately. You will be doing this project, but by yourself. And I will be calling your parents."

"Go ahead and call them," I say. I live with my grandparents and they don't care about anything I do.

"I'll be seeing you," I yell behind my back, "but without my project!"

I rush home to get my black leather jacket, so I can sneak into this rock concert with this fake I.D. On my way, I bump into this really high-class snob from Harvard University.

"Watch where you're going, you big klutz," she says in this British accent I don't like.

So I say, "Have I ever told you that you have an ugly accent?"

"Hmph," she replies and walks away maturely.

When I arrive at the awesome concert, I show the security guard my fake I.D., which claims that I am 21 and my name is Coco Lollipop. Well, I couldn't think of another name, so my name is Coco Lollipop.

The security guard says to me, "Coco Lollipop, huh? Well, that's a weird name, but I'll let ya in."

Woohoo!! I made it!

As I dance into the really awesome concert, I bump into a girl.

"Ow!" she exclaims.

"Sorry," I say real sarcastically. Why would I say sorry to a girl?

She asks me, "What's your name?"

And I answer, "Well, if you must know, my name is Loui Outlaw."

"Hmmm," she says, "Loui Outlaw, sounds familiar."

"Oh yeah? What's your name?"

"The name is Melody Mystery!"

"Mmm, doesn't ring a bell," I say. "Well, bye."

"Wait! I thought I would tell you more about me," she yells. "I am originally from Buffalo, New York."

"Why did you come here?" I ask.

"I came to get my hiking gear from my grandparents."

"What for?" I reply.

"Well, my horse, Ruby, got stolen, so I have to go to Nepal to climb Mount Everest and get her," she says. "I better get going now, see ya."

"Wait! It's Melody, right?" I realize that she could be my first friend, so I should stick with her.

She turns around and says, "Yeah, that's it."

And then I say, "I thought I would come with you to Nepal."

She looks at me as if she knew this was gonna happen, and I say, "My grandparents are too old to care that I'm gone, so let's go."

"Great, wonderful," she says.

"Let's go!" we say together.

And that's when I became a nice person. This was a first. And our adventure together was really fun. But that's a whole different story to tell.

# Zucchini, The Dreaded Curse

*Kelson Ball*

His eyes widened as the large framing hammer rebounded from the soft tissues of his thumb. He choked as screaming pulses of agony ricocheted from one limb to another.

"Zucchini!" he shouted, standing up and howling at the top off his lungs.

In his blind rage he stepped backward, plummeting off the overhanging deck into the river far below.

Inside the ruddy, crawling, cardboard, bison-eyed house a shrill shriek sounded. It had nothing to do with the fall. The screamer already knew that the man was safe. He had fallen in the deep waters of the river, where friendly local salmon would help him swim to safety.

A person doesn't live in a ruddy, crawling, cardboard, bison-eyed house without knowing a thing or two about rivers and the salmon that inhabit them.

No, the scream was a reaction to the word zucchini, which was actually a potent enough curse in a long-forgotten French dialect to curl the hair on a naked mole rat.

The screamer was not a naked mole rat. But still. That kind of curse had to be negated. Falling three stories into a raging river was no excuse for polluting the air with obscenities. Once the man was back on dry land, the screamer intended to have a little chat with him about propriety and wearing a safety harness and swinging his hammer more carefully.

A small girl ran out onto the hot sand just beyond the front door of the ruddy, crawling, cardboard, bison-eyed house and poured a bottle of water on the gawking daisy growing there. The daisy was particularly sensitive to derogative ancient French curses. It sputtered under the flow of water, but stopped gawking.

Satisfied, the girl returned to the ruddy, crawling, cardboard, bison-eyed house.

One of the bison eyes winked. Then, all was still.

# Brains and Blood

*Declan Kimble*

Things couldn't get any worse for me. It was the last day of school. Sophie, Danny, and I were on our way home when Sophie told us a terrible secret.

She was a vampire!

Danny took out his pencil and called it a "wooden stake." I took out my pencil and blocked his strike. We dueled until he screamed, "Jake, do you want the blood sucked out of your body?!" and ran away. I looked back at Sophie, and her mouth was hanging open. The fangs were white and pointy. We walked to our houses in silence. One thought stuck in my mind, though. I needed more turtleneck shirts.

My mom's voice brought me out of my daydream: "Jake, you seem upset. Go watch TV. Get your mind off of whatever is bothering you. Zone out." In the middle of my cartoons I heard: "We interrupt this broadcast to say that local police have found three dead bodies near the graveyard. The coroner performed an autopsy, and he does not know the cause of death, but the brains of the three dead bodies were missing."

*Creak!*

I woke up still wondering why the bullet (from my dream) hadn't hit my skull. What was the creak? I wondered. Out my window I heard a car voosh by. I looked at my clock and saw that it was 12:06 a.m.

Weird. It's either Sophie's parents or someone coming home from Hawaii with black eyeballs and rotten teeth. BLACK EYEBALLS AND ROTTEN TEETH!? I watched too much TV last night! I remember…last night…on TV…

This is what I remembered:

"This is Fred McKleeger, live at Kill Caves. Three dead bodies were found missing their brains. Wha…" Fred looked off screen. "Something's happening! There are some weird figures…they—they—NO…Get away—aaauu—"

The camera showed a silhouette of a figure attacking Fred and…pulling out his brains. Then—static.

I was so tired that I drifted back to sleep.

Things really couldn't get any worse for me.

Right outside the door of the Kandy Head Candy Shop stood Danny with the green humanoid monsters. Maggots crawled on the intestines, wrapped their legs, crawled in and out of their rotten skin, on their torn shirts, around their eyes, and on their sweaty gym socks. Tears dripped out of my eyes as I saw this through the door of the Kandy Head Candy Shop, where I stood, with Sophie.

"I hate the undead," I said instinctively. "Vampires are cool, though," I added quickly, noticing her flinch.

"I know, undead without brains are really annoying," she said, smiling at me.

"Right," I said, smiling back. Then I said, "I have a plan."

Sophie and I gathered supplies as the zombies ate out Danny's brains.

The zombies crawled towards the gumballs I was carrying up to the roof. My trap was set. Danny was still getting eaten, and Sophie and I were now trapped on the roof of the Kandy Head.

"Pass the comics. The zombies will slip right down on

them," I whispered. "They're going down!"

In one second, my aura of confidence went away. Sophie had slipped down into the hordes of zombies.

I was never good at tennis. I just can't hit the ball over the net. But every gumball I hit with my tennis racket knocked off a zombie head. Gumballs lodged in eye sockets. Some even flew up noses.

"Good grief, that was fun," I said, laughing, three days after the zombie attack. People were pretty much fine. Except for Danny. And most of the school bullies.

"Now you could play at Wimbledon and win," Sophie laughed. She was fine, except for a broken arm and a bent fang.

Life was normal again.

# Zombie Apocalypse in Port Salmon

*Ben Griggs*

### Chapter 1

In the peaceful town of Port Salmon, Washington, in the local video game store, Joe Anderson picks up the video game Left 4 Dead. He pays and leaves. He gets into his car to pick up his best friend Max to go target shooting. Max is a businessman who, for some reason, is crazy about guns. Joe is too, but he does it for a living. He tests guns for a leading gun manufacturer. He's always dreamed of becoming the greatest marksman ever.

Max jumps into the car with a briefcase. Joe says, "What's up?" Max opens his briefcase and says, "Check this out." In the briefcase is the new H&K sniper, the latest in sharpshooting technology. "Wow!" says Joe, with a surprised look. "Target practice today is going to be awesome!"

### Chapter 2

Joe gets out of bed after a long night. He grabs a bowl of cereal and walks into the living room to watch TV, but it's all the same on every channel—the same report of "multiple killings, unknown cause of death." To take his mind off the gruesome news on TV, Joe decides to try his new game, which happens to be about the last four people to survive a zombie attack. As he plays, Joe thinks, "Man, this is fun as a game, but I would never want this to happen to me."

He hears groaning noises coming from outside. He walks over to the window and shouts, "Keep it quiet out there!" But little does he know the terrors that await him on the front porch. He opens the front door and on the porch, at his feet, is a mutilated, dead human body. It is his neighbor, Alex! Joe screams in horror. He calls 911 and says, "There is a dead body on my front porch, and it is partially dismembered!" The operator says, "The police will be at your house in fifteen minutes." Joe sits on his couch to wait and tries to relax. He closes his eyes and hears more groaning outside the window. "SHUT UP!!"

## Chapter 3

When Joe wakes up, he sees slaughtered bodies of police scattered on his living room floor. Blood is splashed everywhere. He gets startled and grabs his rifle but realizes he does not have any ammo! He panics and goes into his garage to grab his chain saw. Joe turns around to find a zombie standing in front of him. It has no lips and exposed cheekbones. It wears a ratty shirt and pants. Maggots pour out from its empty left eye socket. By instinct, Joe mows the zombie's head off. A large fountain of blood bursts from its empty neck hole. Joe runs out of the garage to find a horde of zombies standing in front of him. To Joe, they all look the same—sick, disgusting, and targets for his chainsaw. Slash! Rip! Crack!

After hours and hours of splattered arms and various body parts, Joe realizes his friend Max is standing right next to him holding a hammer. As they fight off zombies together, Max yells to Joe, "I thought you could use some help!" Max crushes a zombie's skull, but it's too late. Zombies tear his back open, ripping out his guts. They chow down on his organs. Joe watches in shock—frozen stiff and unable to move. While he is stunned from the brutal massacre of his friend, a zombie walks up wielding a handsaw and saws off Joe's right arm, then his left, and finally his head. Joe's cut-up body lies on the ground gushing blood. It eventually becomes a home for rats and maggots.

Here lies the great soul of Joe Anderson. Let him rest in peace...or not.

# Balloons Were Falling in a Cascade of Colors

# The Honeybee Tree

*Oscar White*

Dear Great Grandma and Grandpa:

Here is a poem I wrote for you in poetry class.

There once was a tree that shined like a honeybee and they called it the honeybee tree. The leaves on the tree were the color of yellow. Everyone in the city called it the Jolly Good Yellow Fellow and that's what they wanted to call it forever and ever. Once the tree got old it started to lose its shell and people tried to help it but the tree didn't get better. But once people started watering it, it started to heal. And people started getting happier. When it turned to fall the yellow leaves started falling off and soon there would be no yellow leaves on the honeybee tree. Except for one called the golden honey leaf and that's how it all ended. The golden honey leaf was still on there.

I hoped you enjoyed the poem.

Love,
Oscar

# The Mombie

*Sean Huberth*

### Chapter 1

Things couldn't get worse for me. I got accused of kicking a kid at school and got sent home early. When I got home I heard the newscaster say, "In other news today, four bodies were found dead at the cemetery. The exact cause of death was unknown, but an autopsy shows that the victims' brains were missing." My mom, who was extremely mad, sent me upstairs. I heard a scream across the street as though someone got hurt, and then out of the corner of my eye I saw a man staggering away from the noise. It was odd but not that much. Then slowly I drifted off to sleep into peaceful dreams.

### Chapter 2

Things got worse for me, a lot worse.

"Come down for breakfast," called my mom. My mom had red curly hair and blue-green eyes. She had bright yellow glasses (in hideous contrast to her eyes). She had light pink earrings. I was standing in my closet when I heard breaking glass, and I told myself not to worry. Her favorite dress was green, blue, chartreuse, baby-poop brown, orange, pink, black, white, red, indigo, violet, fuchsia, magenta, and vomit green. I hustled downstairs to find my mom dead on the floor in her special dress. I felt like I would faint. I was scared. I did not know what to do. She had a bloody head and green slime on her neck. There were muddy footsteps leading to a broken window. I smelled burnt pancakes. I ran to the phone but it wasn't there. I turned on the radio to 103.7 the Mountain, because I am a big fan of Fred McQuiche and I wanted to know if anything else odd was happening in town.

"This is Fred McQuiche, live at the cliffs. Hey what's happening... ah... no... (crash)... ah." I ran to the pay phone outside and dialed 911 as the front door creaked open.

## Chapter 3

I stood at the phone booth and I saw this thing that looked like my mom but a whole lot greener. There were huge, slimy maggots climbing in and out of its mouth. It was foaming at the mouth. Then it started chewing on its intestines. It started toward me. I started running. The dragging of its feet got louder. Then I heard groaning, then I smelled a bad scent of rotting meat. The second I figured out it was a zombie, I tripped and fell into a ditch, had a seizure, and nearly died. When I woke up I was looking at a hospital's white ceiling.

"Lucky you were wearing that zombie-proof hard hat that you got at 826 Port Salmon Zombie Shop or else you could have died," said the doctor.

## Epilogue

And he lived happily ever after, besides the fact that his mom was after him!!

# WATER

*Chloe Noonan*

A difference in every ripple.
A mystery in every ocean.
A danger in every corner.

Water's life is tough and exciting in every way.
Sometimes things happen that make important things drift away.

Don't be mad at Water, it might not be its fault.
Maybe it had a headache or there was something wrong with its salt?

Water may make people and other things disappear forever,
but will Water apologize? Nope, not ever.

Water does not speak at all,
its thoughts drop down into a waterfall.

Is Water lonely? Yes indeed,
all it can talk to is seaweed.

Fish are nice to Water but yet they do not speak.
Fish do not feel like it, not that day or any week.

᛫

Water has workouts, tons of them a day.
Boats are on Water's back, they just function that way.
᛫

Don't feel bad for Water, it's just fine and okay.
You can visit Water any time of every day.

# The S'more-tainous Monster

*Oliver Cauble*

Something was burning in the oven. It was a marshmallow that suddenly (Do! Do! Doo!) ran away because it was hot. Then a storm came by and the marshmallow got struck by lightning. It made it all crisp and yummy—and evil! It began to grow as tall as a house.

Two kids named Conrad and Sally saw the marshmallow. They were surprised, but mostly they were excited to make a giant s'more with it. Conrad and Sally ran home and got two big graham crackers and a chocolate bar. They ran after the marshmallow for hours. They were pretty smart kids, and they had made their own robotic arms to carry heavy things, so they were able to keep running.

The marshmallow didn't see Conrad and Sally at first. It was just running to try to cool down, because the lightning made it hot. The marshmallow climbed the Space Needle, and Conrad and Sally followed it. Neither of them had had a s'more in so long; they wanted the giant marshmallow so badly they didn't even pay attention to how scary it was to climb the Space Needle. The weather was still stormy and the marshmallow got struck by lightning again. It was so swollen now, it started to float up to space.

Conrad and Sally grabbed onto its leg and they were heavy enough to drag it back down. Sally dropped a graham cracker and Conrad dropped the chocolate bar.

They fell for twenty seconds, and the marshmallow landed on top of the chocolate bar. Sally and Conrad put the second graham cracker on top and started jumping on it to squish the marshmallow down. And then they ate it! They put their leftovers in a ginormous plastic bag and dragged them home for later.

# Babette's Tale

*Jasmine Sun*

Babette was digging for food when Buffy, another chicken, went up to her and started talking. "Hey, Babette! Want to play tag?"

Babette thought about this for a moment. It might be fun—she had never really tried—but she wanted more chow. However, she couldn't tell Buffy that! So, she concocted a lie and hoped it would work. "No thanks. My feathers might get dirty."

"Okay," said Buffy. "Join us later if you want."

Buffy seemed kind of disappointed, but she couldn't let that get in the way. Plus, she would get so tired.

"Uh oh," thought Babette. "Here comes Frida."

Frida bullied her constantly. Babette always tried to steer clear of her but it wasn't always possible. Babette tried to run from Frida when she arrived, but Frida was just too fast! Soon, Babette was panting and had to take a rest.

"Ha!" laughed Frida. "You're so fat and lazy that you can only run three feet without having to take a break."

Babette was taken aback. She examined herself, wondering if what Frida said was true. "Well, I am a little on the plump side," thought Babette.

But Frida wasn't finished. "And all you ever do is eat and sleep."

Frida stalked away. Normally, Babette was quite proud

and regal, but her usually glossy feathers suddenly lost their shine.

Babette decided to go to Sally for help. She was patient and kind, not to mention very wise. The other chickens always came to her for advice, and from what Babette had heard, very good advice indeed. She found Sally tending to her five chicks.

"I was wondering what I could do about this—well—um—well—how to lose some weight," said Babette, feeling rather sheepish.

"Mmm hmm …" thought Sally. "Well, you could always try working out!"

"Thanks!" said Babette. "What a good idea! Why didn't I think of that myself?"

So every day, Babette ran and jumped, playing with the other chickens. Soon, she became extremely agile. The next time she had to run from Frida, Babette used all her strength and outran her. For once, Babette left Frida awestruck.

"I can finally, finally outrun Frida!" exclaimed Babette.

Babette was ecstatic and the sheen on her black and white feathers returned. Now Frida couldn't complain about Babette's physical wellness at all! Since Frida now had no one to pick on, she had no choice but to get along with the other chickens. Soon, she and Babette became good friends. Babette was the most energy-filled chicken on the farm.

# Fibonacci: Code of Life and Crime

*Sahl Ali*

It was a bleak Saturday morning in the peaceful city of Bayview. Three men strode into the bank in their crisp, black suits and tinted glasses, holding large briefcases. In unison, they walked with heads held high like dignified gentlemen.

As the watchman greeted them with a "good morning," the three men rudely ignored him.

One by one, the red lights of the security cameras blinked out of existence as the men stopped dead center in the bank. Then the lights went out, and the screaming began. When the lights came back on, the five security guards were gagged and rolling on the floor, as the bank tellers quivered with fear behind the Plexiglas. The three men unveiled their guns from under their jackets and started shoveling bundles of bills into their briefcases in a hurried fashion.

This was not Bill's day; he had woken up on the wrong side of the bed and still hadn't had his daily dose of caffeine. Without his coffee he felt weak, and on top of that, his wife went on a tirade about him not picking up the groceries.

Now his bank was being robbed. Bill wasn't happy. As he pressed the silent alarm button, he wondered how long his wife would yell at him about this.

Another man, dressed in garb similar to the robbers, burst

through the doors yelling, "The police are coming!" One of the robbers took off his sunglasses and stared coldly at the Head of the Bank. Bill could clearly see the long, white scar that extended from the robber's forehead to his lips, and his bald head that contorted as he snarled viciously. Never before had Bill seen such a terrifying figure. The robbers picked up their bags of money and ran out.

No one dared to move inside the bank; they were all too scared. Bill stole a quick glance over his desk and muttered, "Well, that was interesting." Everyone ducked as screeching tires signaled the robbers' escape. Bill calmed everyone, assuring them that the armed robbers had disappeared. He started counting how much money was stolen, counting by the thousands. When he reached $250,000, the police burst in, guns first, and Bill fainted; no one knows if it was from the presence of guns or the large sum of money that was stolen. This was not Bill's day.

* * *

The sun shyly peeked over the cove and illuminated the picturesque beach. The waves gently lapped against the sand, palm trees swaying like dancers as the cool ocean breeze blew the sand. The beach was deserted except for a lone boy, me. I'm Chance, a normal sixteen-year-old boy living in a boring town. My brown hair waved like snakes, and I remembered my mother telling me to get a haircut. Finished with my early morning jog, I walked to the road. Looking both ways, I cautiously took a step forward. Suddenly a black car hurled toward me, careening down the road, speeding without attention. Paralyzed with fear, the smell of burnt rubber wafting into my nose, I saw the driver, a scary looking man with a scar extending from his forehead to his lips. As if I had woken from a dream, I deftly dived to the other side of the road, missing the car by inches. I tried to catch my breath as I noticed a tiny piece of

## 1, 1, 2, 3, 5, 8    U, U, R, R, D, L

I stared at the piece of paper in puzzlement. Then I heard someone call my name, a sweet angelic voice, and my heart stopped again. My good friend Emily emerged from the bushes, gliding gracefully. Emily is my best friend, and no one could ask for a better friend. While I had hordes of mosquitoes following me, she had hordes of boys following her, besotted by her charms. Breathlessly, she exclaimed, "Chance, the bank has been robbed!"

My mouth opened wide with disbelief. Bayview had the lowest crime rate in all of the U.S. It's said that the beautiful views here could melt any criminal's heart. "Is my dad there?" I asked. She briskly nodded and we ran toward the only bank in our city. I had always wanted a little excitement, but never this much.

My dad was a detective, but not just any detective, one of the best ever. I expected my dad to have already found the robbers and put them in jail before we made it to the bank, but I couldn't be more wrong. He grimly greeted Emily and me with a kiss and a handshake. The story he told me made my stomach churn. He explained, "Three armed men robbed the bank and sped off in a black car. We've dispatched helicopters and patrol cars to find them. We were only a few minutes behind them, but it seems that they have vanished off the face of the earth. Dogs can't sniff anything, people haven't seen anything, and no fingerprints were left. If I didn't know better, I'd say a ghost robbed the bank."

"I've seen them," I blurted.

"Excuse me!" said my dad, shocked.

I continued. "I was on the beach finishing my morning jog when I went on Sunview Avenue and a black car almost ran me over."

"Are you okay?" my dad asked worriedly.

"I'm fine, but the windows were tinted, and I only saw a bald man with a long white scar."

My dad murmured, "Fits the description that Bill, the Head of the Bank, gave."

My dad pulled out his radio and barked into it, "All units converge to Sunview Avenue."

I whispered, "Dad, that's not the only thing I saw."

Then my mom came.

Pecking my dad on the cheek and hugging him, she looked around the room searchingly. Slowly but surely, her smile curled downward. I gulped, and Emily left the room to let me face my mom alone. My mom said, "I got a call from your dad." Enunciating each word clearly, as if she was spitting out venom, she asked, "How was your morning jog, sweetie?"

Cheekily, I responded, "It was great! I even practiced gymnastics on the road."

Mom roared, "Don't you talk to me that way! What were you thinking?"

"I was thinking it was a nice day to get run over."

"How many times have I told you to look both ways?"

Under my breath I muttered, "Two thousand times, give or take a hundred."

She screamed at me in frustration. Oops, she wasn't supposed to hear that.

"I'm sorry mom, but it wasn't my fault I almost got hurt badly."

She walked over in tears and choked me in a bear hug.

"Oh, at least my baby is okay," she said, while planting a sloppy kiss on my cheek. I was pretty shaken up by the car, but in my mother's arms I felt safer than ever.

"Mom, Emily is here."

"So? Emily is such a darling, beautiful and smart; plus she doesn't run in front of cars."

My mother, Christina, was the most loving person, but sometimes she was too loving. Sometimes confused with a supermodel, she is the nicest person ever. She's the best mom and I'd never trade her for anything in the world. Emily entered with an impish grin on her lips.

"Christina, I'm sorry but I'm very busy," said my dad.

Bluntly my mom said, "Fine, I won't give you the lunch I made."

"Well, I guess I could take a short break," stammered my dad. So we all had a nice lunch; me, Mom, Dad, and, of course, darling Emily, and we all forgot about the robbery for a few minutes.

After lunch, Emily and I walked to the mall; she said she had to do some shopping and I was her pack mule. At the end of a two-hour shopping spree, with bags in my teeth, I was startled by a phone call and dropped three bags on my poor feet. I yelped while I answered the phone. My dad asked me about what else I saw when I was on Sunview Avenue, so I told him about the scrap of paper and he asked us to come to the station immediately. I told Emily about my dad's call and we ran. Well, actually, Emily ran and I waddled under the weight of twenty shopping bags. I developed a new sense of respect for donkeys that day. I gave the scrap of paper to my dad. He looked at the paper crestfallen and said, "I appreciate your help, but I think all you've found is some lottery numbers. Bye, kids. " I had never seen my dad so pale and haggard. He was even going to sleep at the station. I was worried for Dad. If I ever found the criminals, they would pay.

I turned to Emily and asked, "Do you trust me?"

She replied, "With my life."

Then I said, "I know that this scrap of paper is more important than what my dad said."

"How so?" she asked.

Blushingly, I said, "I don't know."

Emily sighed, "Since you don't know anything, let's review our facts."

"Police were all over the border of the town and they had helicopters. Plus they were only a few minutes behind the robbers. That means the robbers are still in town, only a few minutes away from the bank," I concluded.

"They also went along Sunview Avenue."

"That means they can only be in three possible places then."

Emily gasped in excitement, "The beach, the forest, or the abandoned mines."

"We can rule out the beach, because only an idiot would hide in that open expanse."

Slyly, she rebuked, "Well, they did rob the bank."

"They're still free."

"Fine, let's call them insane."

"That works. That means they're either in the forest or the mines."

"What are we going to do about it?" questioned Emily.

"We're going to go after them."

"Did you take your pills, or are you mad?" she rebuked. "There are two of us, and four of them."

"You take two. I take two. I'm just kidding. We'll just find where they are hiding and tell the police. It's simple."

"Just like all of your other simple plans. We set a record for most detentions in a week because of your so-called simple plans."

"I admit I've made some mistakes."

"Anyway, the abandoned mines and the forest are too big of an area to explore; you can search for years without finding anything."

"You're right, Emily. I'm not thinking this through," I sighed.

She put her hand on my shoulder. "Chance, you're trying to do something really good and I admire it, but we've got to think this out more and I'm sure you'll know what to do."

God, why is she so perfect and nice?

We walked toward the beach. The weather was hot, and there were many people at the beach. We bought ice cream, and I stared at her, thinking how good she looked in front of the beautiful landscape. We walked slowly as our ice cream melted in our mouths. I stared at the seashells and starfish. Then like lightning, I knew what to do. I dropped my ice cream and pulled out the piece of paper. I cried out, "Emily, I know what the numbers are!"

"What is it?" she asked.

"It's the Fibonacci numbers."

In a puzzled voice she asked, "Fiba-who?"

Barely able to contain my joy, I exclaimed, "The Fibonacci numbers, you know, the code to life!"

Exasperated she said, "You're raving like a mad monkey. Explain what you're saying."

I started, "The Fibonacci numbers are special numbers found in the sixth …"

Emily groaned, "Can we please skip the history lesson."

"They start with the numbers zero and one; to find the next number, you add the last two together. What's the next number, Emily?"

"Zero plus one, so the next number is one."

"Next number?"

"One plus one equals two, so the next number is two, then three, then five, then eight, just like the numbers on the paper. I understand, but how does this help?"

I went on with my explanation, "Almost everything in nature is based on the Fibonacci numbers: petals on a flower, number of times a tree branches, number of arms on a starfish, etcetera."

To my dismay Emily wasn't impressed, and said, "Does it show us where to look?"

I replied, "No."

Somberly, she said, "We've learned nothing. It's getting late. I'm going home. Good night."

I watched her leave and my head began to droop. If neither my father nor my best friend believed me, who would? I walked down Sunview Avenue, barely able to perceive the pitch-black forest. I continued my way home, where my mom warmly greeted me. I had my dinner but didn't offer any conversation. I brushed my teeth, kissed my mother goodnight, and trudged into my room. I lay on my bed and stared at the ceiling, pondering the predicament. The forest was the most logical place to hide. With towering trees and the scent of pine to ward off dogs, you could get lost in minutes. Yet, I remembered playing hide and seek with my friends. I always won. Everyone except for me hid in the forest; I hid in the mines.

My mind said forest, but my heart said mines. Sometimes you just have to listen to your heart and let it go. I decided the next day I would search the mines, with or without Emily. I closed my eyes and started to think about what to bring and I drifted into blissful sleep.

I woke up with a start, hearing angry voices downstairs. Were my parents fighting? I quickly brushed my teeth and threw on some clothes to see the commotion. My mother explained in teary eyes that Dad had been fired. There were no leads in the case, and Dad's superiors needed a scapegoat. Even though it had only been a few hours, the mayor was demanding a solution. My father had served faithfully for fifteen years, bringing crime to a standstill, earning himself the reputation of the best detective. In one day, four evil men were able to take away his life's work, like stealing candy from a baby. I wouldn't spare these cruel people.

I went back to my room and started to shove stuff in my backpack. I was going to make sure to make myself ready to meet these sadistic people. I put a flashlight, extra batteries, pocket knife, compass, lighter, walkie-talkies, and a set of binoculars in my bag. Then I went down to the kitchen and made many peanut-butter-and-jelly sandwiches. I gathered all the water bottles I could find. I was ready. I opened the door and was tackled by a flying mass of pink. Emily had come, and had taken me down better than any football player.

She said sheepishly, "Sorry. Didn't know you were there." I gasped, trying to draw back my breath, and was glad that girls didn't play football. I filled her in with everything I knew. Surprisingly, she agreed with my plan of searching and my meaning of the numbers. However, she did tell me that it would be more prudent to figure out what the letters meant first. Looking at our only clue, we started listing words that started with U. We thought of *umbrella*, *under*,

USA, *ugly*. Then it hit us: UP! The U stood for *up*. That meant the D stood for *down*. We had found two of the letters, only two more were left. We agreed it was somehow giving us directions, so we thought of words pertaining to directions that started with an L. *Left*, we exclaimed with excitement! We knew the last letter, R, stood for *right*.

So maybe we had to go up, up, right, right, down, left.

Emily said, "I think the letters and numbers correspond."

I felt like giving her a big hug; we had our breakthrough.

The message was one up, one up, two right, three right, five down, and eight left. If the hideouts were in the tunnels of the mines, the numbers must have told when to make turns in the caves. We were geniuses, and knew where to look. I looked Emily in the eyes and asked, "Do you want to help me find these thieves and bring them to justice?"

She replied saucily, "Only to make sure you don't hurt yourself."

I chuckled. She went back to her house and grabbed similar equipment. We met at the entrance of the cave. I could only see black in there. The mines were called the Maze of Rocks. Not a very poetic name, but a very accurate description. People have died getting lost in the maze. We took a step into the darkness, turning on our flashlights. Emily called, "Together!" I responded, "Always."

We followed the strange directions as the mines unfolded. Bats roamed freely. Their droppings and black swarms proved that much. After two hours, we were on our seventh left. We heard rough voices, obviously arguing.

There were two of them. Voice one yelled, "When can we run with the loot?" Voice two yelled back, "We have to wait; the police are still looking for us."

Suddenly the tip-tap of feet could be heard. The pattering became louder and the person came closer. I saw a rusty pick axe lying on the floor and quickly grabbed it. I waited for the mysterious man. Right as he turned the corner, I brought my makeshift club down, knocking him unconscious. Unfortunately, he let out a loud moan as he went down.

Voice one yelled, "Is that you, Dmitri?"

Voice two yelled even louder, "Shut up, you imbecile, you're not supposed to use our real names. Let's go see what that noise was."

Emily whispered, "Now would be a good time to run."

With a name like Chance, you might think I'm very lucky, but I'm actually not.

As we both ran away, I tripped over some loose stones, hurting my ankle badly. I told Emily to go on but she didn't; she is too good a friend. She stubbornly held her ground and cried, "Together always, remember." As I blacked out, I saw Emily crouched over me very worried. What type of mess did I get us into now?

I opened my eyes, only to see a nightmare. The same man who had robbed the bank, and nearly killed me, was leering over me. The long white scar confirmed that fact. He said, "Well, well. Looks like Prince Charming woke up." His hand went to my throat and he started squeezing. After two minutes, my vision was clouded by flashing lights. When I thought I was going to take my last breath, the cruel man suddenly stopped. Coolly, he said, "You are our prisoner, and if you try to run, I won't stop squeezing next time."

I gulped in fear and watched him walk away. I was tied down and couldn't move my arms or legs. I could roll, but rolling on a bunch of rocks wasn't good for me or my back. I twisted onto my side only to see Emily not a foot away from me, tightly bound. Instantly, my body flooded with relief. At least Emily was safe. She said, "It's funny how your simple plans always get us in deep trouble." I chuckled softly, and I wondered what the criminals were going to do with us.

After an hour, I had learned a lot. The man with the scar was their leader and was nicknamed Boss. Voice two was actually a thin man resembling a rat. He was called Victor. The man we knocked out, who was sitting by a tent with an ice pack held to his head and giving us a murderous look, was named Dmitri. We even saw the fourth person, named Bjorn, who was mainly the lookout. This part of the abandoned mines was supposed to get demolished, but it never happened. Explosives still sat at the edges of the walls.

After another half an hour, Boss barked out orders, "Dmitri and Bjorn, come with me. We're going to get more supplies. Victor stay here! Don't let them out of your sight!" Victor nodded vigorously. Immediately after they left, Victor went to sleep. We were stuck, with no place to go, and could barely move. After twenty minutes, Victor woke up and took out a cigarette and tried unsuccessfully to light it with a broken lighter. He swore. I called out, "I have a lighter." He stared back at me. I continued, "It's in the front pocket of my bag." He grabbed my bag greedily and took out the lighter. He lit his cigarette. Then I asked, "Can I smoke too?" I don't know why, but he let me. He lit another cigarette and was about to hand it to me. I asked, "How am I going to smoke without my hands?" Surprisingly, he untied them. He sat back and enjoyed his cigarette while I rubbed my hands to get the blood circulating again. After being tied up for hours, my hands looked like pale twigs. When he looked, I pretended to smoke. When he wasn't looking, I jabbed the burning end of the cigarette into the rope holding my feet together. Slowly but surely, the rope burned away. After a few minutes, the rope was gone and I was free! I helped out Emily, too, and still Victor hadn't noticed us because we carefully made sure not to show him that we were free. Then Boss and his cronies came back. They looked worried, and started picking up equipment. Boss told Victor, "The police are coming to search the mines."

Hope flared in my body, and I could see that even Emily was smiling.

Victor then said, "They won't be here for another twenty minutes. We have enough time to run and hide again." With that statement, my hopes were dashed again. I had to stall the robbers somehow. My cigarette was still burning, and I was about to stomp it out when Emily kicked me. She stared at me, and then stared at some explosives by the walls, and then stared at the cigarette in my hand. She murmured, "Are you thinking what I'm thinking?"

I hoped that the cigarette was strong enough to light the dynamite. As the four criminals shoved equipment into bags, I crept over to the dynamite. Then I chucked the cigarette into the pile of dynamite. After waiting a few seconds and not hearing anything, I went closer. I thought it wasn't working, but it was! I jumped out of the way, running back to Emily. Boss started yelling wildly at us, still not noticing the lit dynamite. Then thunder sounded, echoing throughout the mines. Orange light filled the atmosphere, looking almost like fireworks. The dynamite worked! Rocks and metals rained down on us. Everyone was screaming. My ears popped. I held Emily in my arms, trying to protect her from the flying rocks. Hit by over a dozen rocks, I finally faltered and blacked out. My last image was the clear night sky. The dynamite had blown a hole clear through the ceiling. The police must be on their way! I blacked out, hoping Emily would be okay.

I woke up in a soft bed. I saw my mother, my father, and Emily. She looked fine except for a few scratches. My mom looked like she had been crying, and so had my dad. They all cried with joy as they hugged and kissed me with delight. Exhausted, I went to sleep again. I woke up in my own house, my father gently shaking me awake. He said that I'd been asleep for almost a day and that there was an award ceremony going on in town for me and Emily that morning. I painfully got dressed in a suit and walked out with my dad.

Everyone in town was gathered, with the mayor beckoning me and Emily onto the stage. Balloons were falling in a cascade of colors and confetti clouded my vision. The mayor gave a speech about how thankful the town was for our actions. Emily and I looked at each other the whole time, grinning from ear to ear. Then he asked what we wanted. I stood up to the microphone and said I wanted my dad to have his job back because he inspired me. The mayor laughed and said, "Don't worry, your dad has already got his job back and has been promoted. He is our best detective!" The mayor continued, "Since you aren't asking for anything, the bank has awarded you each $10,000 for saving their money." Bill strode onto the stage and handed us each a humongous check. My dad and mom came on the stage and we all hugged again. Emily kissed me. The mayor yelled, "Please give a hand for these courageous characters!"

# Afterword

*Megan Burbank, 826 Seattle Programming Intern*

I arrived at 826 Seattle as a summer intern two months after graduating from college in an effort to avoid the plight of being an unemployed 22-year-old with a B.A. in English, and instantly felt as if I had been co-opted into a surreal alternate universe. It wasn't because I sold space travel equipment part-time, although that was weird, but rather because I suddenly found myself sitting in on a summer workshop that used Walt Whitman's "Leaves of Grass" as a springboard for a group of students—some as young as seven—to write songs of themselves.

I was a little confused as to what the end result would be. What do you write about yourself when you're seven? College students are often so distanced from their own childhoods that we think of those still living them as strange, tiny people whose primary purpose in life is to be a source of extreme inconvenience while sporadically looking cute and never understanding sarcasm. But as I listened to the class's culminating reading on their last day at 826, I began to feel kind of like an imposter for calling myself a writer. In a matter of moments, a beautiful honeybee tree had lost all but one leaf, the world was revealed to be a place of both great beauty and great danger, and someone had written a poem comparing humans to machines. If I hadn't been in a dark place of post-grad confusion and existential uncertainty already, this would have gotten me there.

When Samar, my 826 Seattle supervisor, asked me what I thought of the students' pieces, there was only one thing to say: "They're really good. And they're kind of dark."

As parents filed in at the end of class to pick up their kids, one zeroed in on Lucia Minahan's riff on William Carlos Williams, a half-hearted apology for biting her little sister's hand. "What a horrifying little poem by a beautiful little girl," she said.

Well, *duh*, I thought. I would totally have written a poem about biting my brother's hand when I was seven.

And suddenly, something became clear to me. That poem was shocking to an adult reader because it wasn't out to impress anyone or beg for approval. It wasn't hoping for profundity, it didn't care about being interesting or transcendent. It wasn't at all afraid of getting in trouble. The self-consciousness that so often stunts the work of adult writers was nowhere to be found in any of the pieces generated in the poetry class, and it is nowhere to be found in the work in this book. The writing in this book is about the writing.

As the summer progressed, I read stories about mom-eating zombies and crazy fathers on the lam, and the classic quest fable of the Odyssey was re-imagined in the already harrowing halls of a high school, besting Homer with a new layer of hazard and poignancy.

The world described in this book is an imagined one. It is surreal and beautiful, but it makes no effort to avoid the perils of real life. Things fall apart, adults act like children and children are forced to act like adults, heads roll, blood flows, supernatural tragedies pile on top of ordinary problems, and even maple syrup is co-opted into a nefarious scheme. Sometimes the characters respond with courage, and sometimes they just like to be alone. But the writers behind these stories aren't afraid to write into the dark corners of their lives. They aren't easily fooled. We should all be so lucky.

# When a Book Ends in Unbridled Gratitude
## (a page and a half of acknowledgements)

826 Seattle Programs Guru and Gatherer of the Book:
*Kathleen Goldfarb*

Writing Workshops Captain:
*Samar Abulhassan*

Managing Editor, Who Carried Pages of This Book on His Bike:
*Bill Thorness*

Summer 2009 Programs Intern:
*Megan Burbank*

Graphic Designer:
*Julia Littlefield*

Copyeditors:
*Angela J. Fountas, Susan Hodges, Amy Howard, Mi Ae Lipe, Barbara Rotter, Ann Senechal, Paul Swenum*

Workshop Leaders and Their Assistants:
*Elizabeth Alexander, Catherine Bailey, Jordan Beck, Nora Boyd, Eden Benbow, Bill Carty, Loren Drummond, Kevin Emerson, Susan Kostick, Diane Nichols, Jennifer Rainman, Molly Riordan, Jennie Shortridge, Kathy Soren, L. Suzanne Stockman, Elizabeth Umbanhowar, Raphaela Weissman, Zander Winther and Ed Witter*

Tutors Who Provided One-on-One Guidance to the Authors of this Book: *Rebecca Brinson, Janelle Durham, Elena Hershey, David Johnson, Deborah Green, Erin Thompson, Gwen Weinert and Kaitlin Nunn*

(Other) 826 Seattle Staff Who Are the
Spine(s) of Book Odysseys:
*Justin Allan, Alex Allred, Sarah Beecroft, Amelia Boldaji,
Yoko Ott and Devyn Perez*

826 Seattle Board of Directors:
*Sherman Alexie, Jen Belle, David Brotherton, Michele Dunkerley,
Ted Dworkin, Jared Leising, Pam MacEwan, Caroline Maillard,
Shawn Rediger, Tom Robbins and Ann Senechal*

The Person Who Writes the Bright and Scary
and Inspires Kids Throughout the Universe:
*Lemony Snicket*

The Person Who Offers a Gazebo During
Heat Waves or Book Troubles:
*Teri Hein*

# About 826 Seattle

826 Seattle is a nonprofit organization dedicated to supporting students ages 6-18 with their creative and expository writing skills, and to helping teachers inspire their students to write. Our services are structured around our belief that great leaps in learning can happen with one-on-one attention and that strong writing skills are fundamental to future success. With this in mind we provide drop-in tutoring, field trips, after-school workshops, in-school tutoring, help for English language learners, and assistance with student publications. All of our free programs are challenging and enjoyable, and ultimately strengthen each student's power to express ideas effectively, creatively, confidently, and in his or her individual voice.

All donations to 826 Seattle are tax deductible. For more information please visit our web site: www.826seattle.org.